GRE® Exam Advanced Math

Other Kaplan Books Related to Graduate School Admissions:

GRE Exam: Strategies, Practice, and Review

GRE Exam: Premier Live Online

GRE Verbal Workbook

GRE Math Workbook

GRE & GMAT Exams Writing Workbook

GRE Exam Vocabulary in a Box

Get Into Graduate School

GRE® Exam Advanced
Math

PUBLISHING

New York

© 2009 Kaplan, Inc.

Published by Kaplan Publishing, a division of Kaplan, Inc.
1 Liberty Plaza, 24th Floor
New York, NY 10006

Printed in the United States of America

10 9 8 7 6 5 4 3 2 1

ISBN: 978-1-60714-497-7

Table of Contents

About the Expert

Gar Hong is the Lead Instructor at the State College Kaplan Center. He teaches classes and tutors students in Kaplan's LSAT, GRE, GMAT, SAT, DAT, TSS, and GESS courses. He has also written test prep material for the LSAT, GRE, GMAT, SAT, PSAT, ACT, ISEE, SSAT, BMAT, and the UKCAT. Gar was named Kaplan Teacher of the Year in 2005, 2006, and 2008, and was one of seven instructors selected nationally to help create Kaplan's LSAT Advanced course in 2008.

kaptest.com/publishing

The material in this book is up-to-date at the time of publication. However, the Educational Testing Service may have instituted changes in the test after this book was published. Be sure to carefully read the materials you receive when you register for the test.

If there are any important late-breaking developments—or any changes or corrections to the Kaplan test preparation materials in this book—we will post that information online at **kaptest.com/publishing**. Check to see if there is any information posted there regarding this book.

kaplansurveys.com/books

We'd love to hear your comments and suggestions about this book. We invite you to fill out our online survey form at **kaplansurveys.com/books**. Your feedback is extremely helpful as we continue to develop high-quality resources to meet your needs.

The Perfect Score

Ah, *perfection* . . . We humans are a demanding bunch. We don't bound out of bed in the morning aspiring to mediocrity, but rather striving for *perfection*. The *perfect* mate. The *perfect* job. The *perfect* shoes to go with the *perfect* outfit.

Webster's defines *perfection* as "the quality or state of being complete and correct in every way, conforming to a standard or ideal with no omissions, errors, flaws or extraneous elements." The GRE test makers define perfection as a score of 800. If GRE perfection is what you're after, then you've come to the right place. Kaplan has been training test takers to ace the GRE for decades, and we salute your quest for perfection. The *perfect* GRE score. The *perfect* business school. The *perfect* career. We have the *perfect* book for you.

ABOUT THE GRE

Let's take a look at the current GRE. As someone famous once said, "Know thine enemy." And you need to know firsthand the way this test is put together if you want to take it apart. Before you begin, though, remember that the test makers sometimes change the content, administration, and scheduling of the GRE too quickly for a published guide to keep up with. For the latest, up-to-the-minute news about the GRE, visit Kaplan's website at **kaptest.com**.

The GRE is a test that is designed to assess readiness for graduate school for a wide variety of programs. The ways in which graduate schools use GRE scores vary. Scores are often used as part of the application packet for entrance into a program, but they can also be used to grant fellowships or financial aid.

The GRE is administered on computer and is between two and three-quarters and three and a quarter hours long. The exam consists of three scored sections, with different amounts of time allotted for you to complete each section.

Verbal	
Time	30 minutes
Length	30 multiple-choice questions
Format	Sentence Completion, Analogy, Reading Comprehension, and Antonym
Content	Tests vocabulary, verbal reasoning skills, and the ability to read complex passages with understanding and insight

Quantitative	
Time	45 minutes
Length	28 multiple-choice questions
Format	Quantitative Comparison, Word Problems, and Data Interpretation (graph questions)
Content	Tests basic mathematical skills, ability to understand and apply mathematical concepts, and quantitative reasoning skills

Analytical Writing	
Time	75 minutes
Length	2 essay prompts
Format	Perspective on an Issue and Analyze an Argument
Content	Tests ability to understand and analyze arguments, to understand and draw logical conclusions, and to write clearly and succinctly

The Verbal and Quantitative sections each yield a scaled score within a range of 200 to 800. These scaled scores are like the scores that you received if you took the SAT. You cannot score higher than 800 on either section, no matter how hard you try. Similarly, it's impossible (again, no matter how hard you try) to get a score lower than 200 on either section.

But you don't receive *only* scaled scores. You will also receive a percentile rank, which will place your performance relative to those of a large sample population of other GRE takers. Percentile scores tell graduate schools just what your scaled scores are worth, in a large pool of applicants.

For complete GRE registration information, visit the Educational Testing Service at **gre.org** for the Registration Bulletin.

WHO SHOULD USE THIS BOOK

This book is comprised exclusively of examples of the toughest material you're likely to see on the GRE. No easy stuff, no run-of-the-mill strategies—just killer problems, passages, and questions, complete with Kaplan's proven techniques to help you transcend "above average" and enter the rarefied arena of GRE elite. Even if a perfect score is not your immediate goal, diligent practice with the difficult material in this book can help develop your skills and raise your score. If you're looking for more traditional practice for the GRE, then we recommend working through *Kaplan GRE Exam Premier Live Online* or *Kaplan GRE Exam Strategies, Practice, and Review* books as a prerequisite for the highly challenging material contained in this volume. You can find the latest edition of these books in stores nationwide, as well as by visiting us at kaplanpublishing.com or through other online retailers.

HOW TO USE THIS BOOK

This book is divided into sections corresponding to the quantitative skills and question types contained on the GRE. Jump right to the section that gives you the most trouble, or work through the sections in the order presented—it's up to you. No matter what you do, try not to overload; remember that this is dense, complicated material and not representative of the range of difficulty you'll see on Test Day. One thing's for sure: if you can ace this stuff, the real thing will be a breeze.

Good luck!

A Special Note for International Students

About 250,000 international students pursue advanced academic degrees at the master's or PhD level at U.S. universities each year. This trend of pursuing higher education in the United States, particularly at the graduate level, is expected to continue. Business, management, engineering, and the physical and life sciences are popular areas of study for international students. If you are an international student planning on applying to a graduate program in the United States, you will want to consider the following:

- If English is not your first language, you will probably need to take the Test of English as a Foreign Language (TOEFL®) or show some other evidence that you're proficient in English prior to gaining admission to a graduate program. Graduate programs will vary on what is an acceptable TOEFL score. For degrees in business, journalism, management, or the humanities, a minimum TOEFL score of 600 (250 on the computer-based TOEFL) or better is expected. For the hard sciences and computer technology, a TOEFL score of 550 (213 on the computer-based TOEFL) is a common minimum requirement.

- You may also need to take the Graduate Record Exam (GRE®) or the Graduate Management Admissions Test (GMAT®) as part of the admission process.

- Since admission to many graduate programs and business schools is quite competitive, you may want to select three or four programs you would like to attend and complete applications for each program.

- Selecting the correct graduate school is very different from selecting an undergraduate school. You should research the qualifications and interests of faculty members teaching and doing research in your chosen field. Also, select a program that meets your current or future employment needs, rather than simply a program with a big name.

- Begin the application process at least a year in advance. Be aware that many programs offer only August or September start dates. Find out application deadlines and plan accordingly.

- Finally, you will need to obtain a 1-20 Certificate of Eligibility in order to obtain an F-1 Student Visa to study in the United States.

Kaplan English Programs*

If you need more help with the complex process of graduate school admissions or assistance preparing for the TOEFL, GRE, or GMAT, you may be interested in Kaplan's programs for international students. Kaplan English Programs were designed to help students and professionals from outside the United States meet their educational and career goals. At locations throughout

*Kaplan is authorized under federal law to enroll nonimmigrant alien students.
Kaplan is accredited by ACCET (Accrediting Council for Continuing Education and Training).

the United States, international students take advantage of Kaplan's programs to help them improve their academic and conversational English skills, raise their scores on the TOEFL, GRE, GMAT, and other standardized exams, and gain admission to top programs.

General Intensive English

Kaplan's General Intensive English classes are designed to help you improve your skills in all areas of English and to increase your fluency in spoken and written English. Classes are available for beginning to advanced students, and the average class size is 12 students.

TOEFL and Academic English

This course provides you with the skills you need to improve your TOEFL score and succeed in an American university or graduate program. It includes advanced reading, writing, listening, grammar, and conversational English. You will also receive training for the TOEFL using Kaplan's exclusive computer-based practice materials.

GRE for International Students

The Graduate Record Exam (GRE) is required for admission to many graduate programs in the United States. Nearly one-half million people take the GRE each year. A high score can help you stand out from other test takers. This course, designed especially for non-native English speakers, includes the skills you need to succeed on each section of the GRE, as well as access to Kaplan's exclusive computer-based practice materials and extra verbal practice.

GMAT for International Students

The Graduate Management Admissions Test (GMAT) is required for admission to many graduate programs in business in the United States. Hundreds of thousands of American students have taken this course to prepare for the GMAT. This course, designed especially for non-native English speakers, includes the skills you need to succeed on each section of the GMAT, as well as access to Kaplan's exclusive computer-based practice materials and extra verbal practice.

Other Kaplan Programs

Since 1938, more than three million students have come to Kaplan to advance their studies, prepare for entry to American universities, and further their careers. In addition to the above programs, Kaplan offers courses to prepare for the SAT®, LSAT®, MCAT®, DAT®, USMLE®, NCLEX®, and other standardized exams at locations throughout the United States.

To get more information or to apply to any of Kaplan's programs, contact us at:

Kaplan English Programs
700 S. Flower, Suite 2900
Los Angeles, CA 90017 USA
Phone (if calling from within the United States): 800-818-9128
Phone (if calling from outside the United States): (213) 452-5800
Fax: (213) 892-1364
Website: www.kaplanenglish.com
Email: world@kaplan.com

section one

STRAIGHT MATH PRACTICE

CHAPTER ONE

Arithmetic

Here in the arithmetic section, you'll find problems dealing with percents, exponents and radicals, number properties, rates and ratios, and generally tricky arithmetic to give you extra challenging practice. Then we'll see how they can help to rack up points on the most difficult arithmetic questions.

Two topics you should focus on especially for the GRE are number properties and roots and exponents. Roots and exponents are just plain tough. Number properties questions are also tough because they test information no one ever uses, such as prime numbers, odd and even numbers, etc. It may seem like math trivia from eighth grade, but the GRE considers it very important.

PERCENTS PRACTICE SET

1. If a television is sold at a 25% profit, what percent of the sale price is the profit?

   (A) 5%

   (B) $16\frac{2}{3}$%

   (C) 20%

   (D) 25%

   (E) $33\frac{1}{3}$%

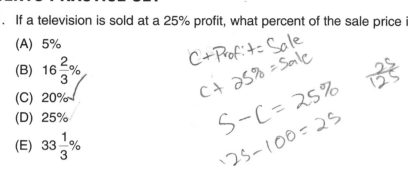

2. If the value of a number increased by 30% is 280, what is the value of that number decreased by 35%?

   (A)   65

   (B)   82

   (C)   98

   (D)   140

   (E)   182

3. The price of a refrigerator decreases by 20% and then by 25%. By what percent must the price increase to reach the original price?

   (A) $33\frac{1}{3}$%

   (B) 40%

   (C) 45%

   (D) $66\frac{2}{3}$%

   (E) 75%

EXPONENTS & RADICALS

4. $27^{-\frac{2}{3}} + 25^{\frac{3}{2}} - 3^{-2} =$

   (A) 2^2

   (B) 3^2

   (C) 3^3

   (D) 5^2

   (E) 5^3 ✓

5. $\dfrac{4\sqrt{6}}{5\sqrt{2}} \times \dfrac{7\sqrt{5}}{\sqrt{10}} \div \dfrac{8\sqrt{2}}{4\sqrt{8}} =$

   (A) $\dfrac{8\sqrt{6}}{15}$

   (B) $\dfrac{15\sqrt{3}}{13}$

   (C) $\dfrac{15\sqrt{19}}{13}$

   (D) $\dfrac{19\sqrt{13}}{18}$

   (E) $\dfrac{28\sqrt{6}}{5}$ ✓

6. $\dfrac{3 \times 16^3 - 8^3 \times 5}{4^4} =$

   (A) 24

   (B) 38 ✓

   (C) 46

   (D) 58

   (E) 74

KAPLAN

AVERAGES

7. The average (arithmetic mean) of 12 numbers is 12. If 8 is subtracted from each of 8 of the numbers and 4 is added to each of the remaining 4 numbers, what is the new average?

   (A) 3
   (B) 4
   (C) 6
   (D) 8
   (E) 9

8. The average (arithmetic mean) of eight numbers is 14. If the average of three of these numbers is 4, what is the average of the remaining five numbers?

   (A) 17
   (B) 18
   (C) 20
   (D) 23
   (E) 26

9. The average (arithmetic mean) of a, b, 9, 10, and 11 is 10. If $ab = 56$ and $b > a$, then $a =$

   (A) 2
   (B) 5
   (C) 7
   (D) 8
   (E) 11

NUMBER PROPERTIES

10. If the sum of five distinct negative integers is –15, then the greatest of these integers is

    (A) –1
    (B) –2
    (C) –3
    (D) –4
    (E) –5

11. Which one of the following is NOT a factor of 15^{51}?

    (A) 25
    (B) 27
    (C) 35
    (D) 81
    (E) 125

12. If f is positive and g is negative, which of the following must be negative?

    (A) $f - g$
    (B) $f + g$
    (C) $fg + 3$
    (D) $-(f + g)^2$
    (E) $-|f - g|$

RATIOS & RATES

13. Set *M* has 2 prime numbers for every 5 composite numbers. If set *M* has 280 numbers, how many more numbers are composite than prime?

    (A) 40
    (B) 80
    (C) 120
    (D) 200
    (E) 240

14. Maria's fruit punch is half water and half punch. If adding 24 ounces of water changes the water-to-punch ratio to 7:5, how many ounces of punch are there?

    (A) 5
    (B) 10
    (C) 24
    (D) 36
    (E) 60

15. Skiing down a 120-meter slope takes 20 seconds. If climbing back up is done at a rate of 180 meters per minute, what is the average speed, in meters per second, for the round-trip?

    (A) 4
    (B) 4.5
    (C) 24
    (D) 60
    (E) 93

ADVANCED ARITHIMETIC

16. The population of a certain town increases by 50 percent every 50 years. If the population in 1950 was 810, in what year was the population 160?

    (A) 1650
    (B) 1700
    (C) 1750
    (D) 1800
    (E) 1850

17. Five percent of a certain grass seed is timothy. If the amount of the mixture needed to plant one acre contains 2 pounds of timothy, how many acres can be planted with 240 pounds of the seed mixture?

    (A) 6
    (B) 12
    (C) 20
    (D) 24
    (E) 120

18. A brush salesman earns $50 salary each month plus 10 percent commission on the value of his sales. If he earned $200 last month, what was the total value of his sales?

    (A) $1,000
    (B) $1,200
    (C) $1,500
    (D) $2,000
    (E) $2,500

19. A man bought 10 crates of oranges for $80 total. If he lost 2 of the crates, at what price would he have to sell each of the remaining crates in order to earn a total profit of 25 percent of the total cost?

    (A) $10.00
    (B) $12.50
    (C) $15.00
    (D) $100.00
    (E) $120.00

20. Which of the following is (are) equal to 8^5?
    I. $2^5 \cdot 4^5$
    II. 2^{15}
    III. $2^5 \cdot 2^{10}$

    $2^5 \cdot (2^2)^5$ $8^5 = (2^3)^5 = 2^{15}$

    (A) II only
    (B) I and II only
    (C) I and III only
    (D) II and III only
    (E) I, II, and III

21. If $27n = 9^4$, then $n =$
    (A) $\dfrac{4}{3}$
    (B) 2
    (C) $\dfrac{8}{3}$
    (D) 3
    (E) 8

    $27^n = 9^4$

    $(3 \cdot 3^2)^n = 9^4$

    $3^{3n} = (3^2)^4$

    $3^{3n} = 3^8$

22. If $xyz \neq 0$, then
    (A) x^2y^3z
    (B) $x^4y^{-1}z^7$
    (C) $x^2y^{-1}z$
    (D) $x^2y^3z^2$
    (E) x^2yz

23. If line segments AB and CD have lengths of $10 + \sqrt{7}$ and $5 - \sqrt{7}$ respectively, AB is greater than CD by how much?
    (A) $5 - 2\sqrt{7}$
    (B) $5 + 2\sqrt{7}$
    (C) $15 + 2\sqrt{7}$
    (D) 5
    (E) 15

    $10 + \sqrt{7} - 5 + \sqrt{7}$

    $5 + 2\sqrt{7}$

24. If $x^a \cdot x^b = 1$ and $x \neq \pm 1$, then $a + b =$
    (A) x
    (B) -1
    (C) 0
    (D) 1
    (E) It cannot be determined from the information given.

    $x^{a+b} = 1$

    $x^0 = 1$

25. An alloy of tin and copper has six pounds of copper for every two pounds of tin. If 200 pounds of this alloy are made, how many pounds of tin are required?

    (A) 25
    (B) 50
    (C) 100
    (D) 125
    (E) 150

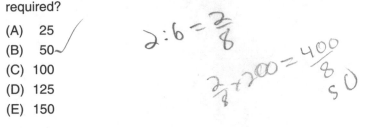

26. A sporting goods store ordered an equal number of white and yellow tennis balls. The tennis ball company delivered 30 extra white balls, making the ratio of white balls to yellow balls 6:5. How many tennis balls did the store originally order?

    (A) 120
    (B) 150
    (C) 180
    (D) 300
    (E) 330

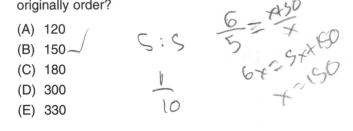

27. If $a = 2b$, $\frac{1}{2}b$, and $4c = 3d$, then what is the ratio of d to a?

    (A) $\frac{1}{3}$

    (B) $\frac{3}{4}$

    (C) 1

    (D) $\frac{4}{3}$

    (E) 3

28. An optometrist charges $30.00 for an eye examination, frames, and glass lenses, but $42.00 for an eye examination, frames, and plastic lenses. If the plastic lenses cost four times as much as the glass lenses, how much do the glass lenses cost?

    (A) $2
    (B) $4
    (C) $5
    (D) $6
    (E) $8

29. If $\frac{1}{2}$ of the number of white mice in a certain laboratory is $\frac{1}{8}$ of the total number of mice, and $\frac{1}{3}$ of the number of gray mice is $\frac{1}{9}$ of the total number of mice, then what is the ratio of white mice to gray mice?

    (A) 16:27
    (B) 2:3
    (C) 3:4
    (D) 4:5
    (E) 8:9

30. If the product of two integers is an even number and the sum of the same two integers is an odd number, which of the following must be true?

    (A) The two integers are both odd.
    (B) The two integers are both even.
    (C) One of the two integers is odd and the other is even.
    (D) One of the integers is 1.
    (E) The two integers are consecutive.

31. If both the product and sum of four integers are even, which of the following could be the number of even integers in the group?

    I.   0
    II. 2
    III. 4

    (A) I only
    (B) II only
    (C) III only
    (D) II and III only
    (E) I, II, and III

32. A wire is cut into three equal parts. The resulting segments are then cut into 4, 6, and 8 equal parts respectively. If each of the resulting segments has an integer length, what is the minimum length of the wire?

    (A) 24
    (B) 36
    (C) 48
    (D) 54
    (E) 72

33. How many positive integers less than 60 are equal to the product of a positive multiple of 5 and an even number?

   (A) Four
   (B) Five
   (C) Nine
   (D) Ten
   (E) Eleven

34. If the average (arithmetic mean) of 18 consecutive odd integers is 534, then the least of these integers is

   (A) 517
   (B) 518
   (C) 519
   (D) 521
   (E) 525

35. During one week, a stock closed at $75.58 on Monday, $75.63 on Tuesday, $75.42 on Wednesday, and $75.52 on Thursday. If the average (arithmetic mean) closing price for the five days was $75.50, what was the closing price on Friday?

   (A) $75.35
   (B) $75.40
   (C) $75.42
   (D) $75.45
   (E) $75.48

36. The average (arithmetic mean) of six positive numbers is 5. If the average of the least and greatest of these numbers is 7, what is the average of the other four numbers?

   (A) 3
   (B) 4
   (C) 5
   (D) 6
   (E) 7

37. If the average (arithmetic mean) of a, b, and 7 is 13, what is the average of $a + 3$, $b - 5$, and 6?

   (A) 7
   (B) 9
   (C) 10
   (D) 12
   (E) 16

ARITHMETIC PRACTICE SET ANSWER KEY

1.	C		20.	E
2.	D		21.	C
3.	D		22.	D
4.	E		23.	B
5.	E		24.	C
6.	B		25.	B
7.	D		26.	D
8.	C		27.	A
9.	A		28.	B
10.	A		29.	C
11.	C		30.	C
12.	E		31.	D
13.	C		32.	E
14.	E		33.	B
15.	A		34.	A
16.	C		35.	A
17.	A		36.	B
18.	C		37.	D
19.	B			

EXPLANATIONS

1. With no number for the original price of the television, you should pick numbers. (For a detailed explanation of the "picking numbers" strategy, see the chapter on word problems.) Since we're dealing with percents, pick 100 for the original price. A $100 television sold at a 25% profit has a selling price of $100 × 1.25 = $125 and a profit of $125 − $100 = $25. The profit is $\dfrac{\$25}{\$125} = \dfrac{1}{5}$ of the sale price, or 20%.

2. You *could* just crunch the numbers, but it's a lot quicker and easier to see what increasing by 30% and decreasing by 35% does to a number. Let's ignore the 280 for now and pick 100 for the number. If you increased 100 by 30%, you'd have 100 + 30 = 130. If you instead decreased 100 by 35%, you'd have 100 − 35 = 65. 130 is twice 65, so the 280 in the question stem must be twice the value of the correct answer. That's choice (D).

3. Be wary of the multiple percent trap on the GRE: the cumulative percent change is never the sum of those changes. Since our fridge has no known price, pick 100 for the original price. The first decrease of 20% would bring the price down to 100 − .20(100) = 100 − 20 = 80. The second decrease of 25% would bring the price down to 80 − .25(80) = 80 − 20 = 60. To go from 60 back to 100 requires an increase of 100 − 60 = 40, which is a $\dfrac{40}{60} = \dfrac{2}{3} = 66\dfrac{2}{3}\%$ increase.

4. A great way to work with fractional exponents is to first convert them into radical form:

$$27^{-\frac{2}{3}} + 25^{\frac{3}{2}} - 3^{-2} = \dfrac{1}{27^{\frac{2}{3}}} + (\sqrt{25})^3 - \dfrac{1}{3^2}$$

$$= \left(\dfrac{1}{\sqrt[3]{27}}\right)^2 + 5^3 - \dfrac{1}{9}$$

$$= \left(\dfrac{1}{3}\right)^2 + 125 - \dfrac{1}{9}$$

$$= \dfrac{1}{9} + 125 - \dfrac{1}{9}$$

$$= 125$$

$$= 5^3$$

5. Radicals may *look* intimidating (the math ones seem pretty scary too!), but basic operations are still performed the same way. The only thing you need to remember is to not leave any radicals in the denominator.

$$\frac{4\sqrt{6}}{5\sqrt{2}} \times \frac{7\sqrt{5}}{\sqrt{10}} \div \frac{8\sqrt{2}}{4\sqrt{8}} = \frac{4\sqrt{6}}{5\sqrt{2}} \times \frac{7\sqrt{5}}{\sqrt{10}} \times \frac{4\sqrt{8}}{8\sqrt{2}}$$

$$= \frac{4\sqrt{3}(\sqrt{2})}{5\sqrt{2}} \times \frac{7\sqrt{5}}{\sqrt{2}(\sqrt{5})} \times \frac{4(\sqrt{4})(\sqrt{2})}{8\sqrt{2}}$$

$$= \frac{4\sqrt{3}}{5} \times \frac{7}{\sqrt{2}} \times \frac{8}{8}$$

$$= \frac{28\sqrt{3}}{5\sqrt{2}}$$

$$= \frac{28\sqrt{3}}{5\sqrt{2}} \times \frac{\sqrt{2}}{\sqrt{2}}$$

$$= \frac{28\sqrt{6}}{5}$$

6. Since all of the exponential terms have base 2 in common, begin by converting them to this common base:

$$\frac{3 \times 16^3 - 8^3 \times 5}{4^4} = \frac{3 \times (2^4)^3 \times (2^3)^3 \times 5}{(2^2)^4}$$

$$= \frac{3 \times 12^{12} - 2^9 \times 5}{2^8}$$

Now split the fraction at the minus sign and solve:

$$\frac{3 \times 2^{12}}{2^8} - \frac{2^9 \times 5}{2^8} = 3 \times 2^4 - 2^1 \times 5$$

$$= 3 \times 16 - 2 \times 5$$

$$= 48 - 10$$

$$= 38$$

7. If the average of 12 numbers is 12, their sum is $12 \times 12 = 144$. Subtracting 8 from each of 8 numbers subtracts $8 \times 8 = 64$ from the sum, leaving $144 - 64 = 80$. Adding 4 to each of 4 numbers adds $4 \times 4 = 16$ to the sum, resulting in a new sum of $80 + 16 = 96$. Twelve numbers that sum to 96 have an average of $96 \div 12 = 8$.

8. When an average problem seems difficult to approach, try working with the sum instead. Eight numbers with an average of 14 have a sum of $8 \times 14 = 112$. Three of these numbers have an average of 4, so their sum is $3 \times 4 = 12$. That leaves a sum of $112 - 12 = 100$ for the remaining five numbers, which comes out to an average of $100 \div 5 = 20$.

9. Five numbers with an average of 10 have a sum of $5 \times 10 = 50$. Three of the numbers are 9, 10, and 11, so the remaining two have a sum of $50 - (9 + 10 + 11) = 50 - 20 = 30$. You are told that $ab = 56$. The only two factors of 56 with a sum of 30 are 2 and 28. Since $b > a$, a must be 2.

10. If five distinct negative integers sum to -15, the five integers must be -1, -2, -3, -4, and -5. Watch out for trap choice (E)—negative numbers *decrease* in value as their absolute value gets larger. The greatest of the integers is -1, which is choice (A).

11. Evaluating 15^{51} and then dividing each choice into it would take even an advanced test taker more time than you have on the GRE. So don't do it that way. The easiest way to find the odd man out is through prime factorization. 15's prime factors are 3 and 5, and the size of the exponent relative to the size of the choices ensures that there are more than enough 3s and 5s to go around. Let's see what happens when we prime factor the choices:

    (A) $25 = 5 \times 5$

    (B) $27 = 3 \times 3 \times 3$

    (C) $35 = 5 \times 7$

    (D) $81 = 3 \times 3 \times 3 \times 3$

    (E) $125 = 5 \times 5 \times 5$

    Choice (C) requires a prime factor of 7. No matter how many 15s there are, you will never be able to factor a 7 out of it, so (C) is correct.

12. With variables all over the place, this problem is perfect for picking numbers. Try 1 for f and -1 for g:

    (A) $1 - (-1) = 1 + 1 = 2$. Eliminate.
    (B) $1 + (-1) = 1 - 1 = 0$. Eliminate.
    (C) $1(-1) + 3 = -1 + 3 = 2$. Eliminate.
    (D) $-(1 + (-1))^2 = -(1 - 1)^2 = -0^2 = 0$. Eliminate.
    (E) $-|1 - (-1)| = -|1 + 1| = -|2| = -2$. Keep this.

    Only (E) works, so it must be correct.

13. In ratio problems, it's important to distinguish the parts from the whole. Set M has 2 primes for every 5 composites, so the part:part ratio is 2:5, and the whole is $2 + 5 = 7$. The 280 numbers represent this whole, so "one part" is $280 \div 7 = 40$ numbers. That means there are $2 \times 40 = 80$ prime numbers and $5 \times 40 = 200$ composite numbers, and their difference is $200 - 80 = 120$.

14. The original ratio of water to punch is 5:5. Adding 24 ounces of water changes this ratio to 7:5, so those 24 ounces of water must represent 7 − 5 = 2 parts water and each part is 24 ÷ 2 = 12 ounces. The mixture has five parts punch, or 12 × 5 = 60 ounces.

15. Be careful not to read too quickly on the GRE: the second rate is given in meters per *minute*, so convert 180 meters per minute to 3 meters per second before proceeding. The downhill trip takes 20 seconds while the uphill trek takes $\dfrac{120\ meters}{3\ meters\ per\ second}$ = 40 seconds. That's a total of 20 + 40 = 60 seconds for a 120 + 120 = 240 meters, so the average speed is $\dfrac{240\ meters}{60\ second}$ = 4 meters per second.

16. Since the population increases by 50% every 50 years, the population in 1950 was 150%, or $\dfrac{3}{2}$ of the 1900 population. This means the 1900 population was $\dfrac{2}{3}$ of the 1950 population. Similarly, the 1850 population was $\dfrac{2}{3}$ of the 1900 population, and so on. We can just keep multiplying by until we get to a population of 160.

    The population was 160 in 1750.

17. 5% of the total mixture is timothy (a type of grass) so, to find the amount of timothy, we use % timothy × whole = amount of timothy. Thus, the amount of timothy in 240 pounds of mixture is 5% − 240 pounds, or 12 pounds. If 12 pounds of timothy are available and each acre requires 2 pounds, then $\dfrac{12}{2}$ or 6 acres can be planted.

18. The commission earned was $200, less the $50 salary, or $150. This represents 10% of his total sales, or of his total. Since this is $\dfrac{1}{10}$ of the total, the total must be 10 times as much, or 10 × $150 = $1,500.

19. The man paid $80 for 10 crates of oranges, and then lost 2 crates. That leaves him with 8 crates. We want to find the price per crate that will give him an overall profit of 25%. First, what is 25% or $80? It's $20. So to make a 25% profit, he must bring in ($80 + $20) or $100 in sales receipts. If he has 8 crates, that means that each crate must sell for $100/8, or $12.50.

20. This question is a good review of the rules for the product of exponential expressions. In order to make the comparison easier, try to transform 85 and each of the three options so that they have a common base. Since 2 is the smallest base among the expressions to be compared, let it be our common base. Since $8^5 = (2^3)^5 = 2^{3 \cdot 5} = 2^{15}$, we will look for options equivalent to 2^{15}.

    I. $2^5 \cdot 4^5 = 2^5 \cdot (2^2)^5 = 2^5 \cdot 2^{2 \cdot 5} = 2^5 \cdot 2^{10} = 2^{5+10} = 2^{15}$ OK

    II. 2^{15} OK

    III. $2^5 \cdot 2^{10} = 2^{5+10} = 2^{15}$ OK

    It turns out that all three are equivalent to 2^{15} or 8^5.

21. The simplest approach is to express both 9 and 27 as an exponent with a common base. The most convenient base is 3, since $3^2 = 9$ and $3^3 = 27$. Then the equation becomes:

$$27^n = 9^4$$
$$(3^3)^n = (3^2)^4$$
$$3^{3 \times n} = 3^{2 \times 4}$$
$$3^{3n} = 3^8$$

If two terms with the same base are equal, the exponents must be equal.

22. First let's break up the expression to separate the variables, transforming the fraction into a product of three simpler fractions:

Now carry out each division by keeping the base and subtracting the exponents. The answer is the product of these three expressions, or $x^2 y^3 z$.

23. Subtract the length of *CD* from the length of *AB* to find out how much greater *AB* is than *CD*.

$$AB - CD = (10 + \sqrt{7}) - (5 - \sqrt{7})$$
$$= 10 + \sqrt{7} - 5 - (-\sqrt{7})$$
$$= 10 - 5 + \sqrt{7} + \sqrt{7}$$
$$= 5 + 2\sqrt{7}$$

24. We are told that and $x^a \cdot x^b = 1$. Since x^{a+b}, we know that $x^{a+b} = 1$. If a power is equal to 1, either the base is 1 or −1, or the exponent is zero. Since we are told $x \neq 1$ or −1 here, the exponent must be zero; therefore, $a + b = 0$.

25. Every 8 pounds of the alloy has six pounds of copper and two pounds of tin. Therefore, $\frac{2}{8}$ or $\frac{1}{4}$ of the alloy is tin. To make 200 pounds of the alloy, we need $\frac{1}{4} \times 200$ or 50 pounds of tin.

26. We can solve this algebraically. Let the number of yellow balls received be x. Then the number of white balls received is 30 more than this, or $x + 30$.

So $\dfrac{\text{\# of white balls}}{\text{\# of yellow balls}} = \dfrac{6}{5} = \dfrac{x + 30}{x}$

Cross-multiply: $6x = 5(x + 30)$

Solve for x: $6x = 5x + 150$

$$x = 150$$

Since the number of white balls ordered equals the number of yellow balls ordered, the total number of balls ordered is $2x$, which is 2×150, or 300.

We could also solve this more intuitively.

The store originally ordered an equal number of white and yellow balls; they ended up with a white to yellow ratio of 6:5. This means for every 5 yellow balls, they got 6 white balls, or they got more white balls than yellow balls. The difference between the number of white balls and the number of yellow balls is just the 30 extra white balls they got. So 30 balls represents $\frac{1}{5}$ of the number of yellow balls. Then the number of yellow balls is 5 × 30 or 150. Since they ordered the same number of white balls as yellow balls, they also ordered 150 white balls, for a total order of 150 + 150 or 300 balls.

27. **Method I:**

We want to eliminate the b's and c's. We start with $a = 2b$. Since, we see that $b = 2c$, then $a = 2(2c) = 4c$. But $4c = 3d$, which means that $a = 3d$. If a is 3 times d, then $\frac{a}{d} = \frac{3}{1}$, or $\frac{d}{a} = \frac{1}{3}$.

Method II:

We're looking for the ratio of d to a, or in other words, the value of the fraction $\frac{d}{a}$. Notice that we can use successive cancellations and write: $\frac{d}{a} = \frac{\cancel{b}^{1}}{a} \times \frac{\cancel{c}^{1}}{\cancel{b}^{1}} \times \frac{d}{\cancel{c}^{1}}$.

Find values for each of the fractions $\frac{b}{a}$, $\frac{c}{b}$ and $\frac{d}{c}$.

$a = 2b$, so $\frac{b}{a} = \frac{1}{2}$

$\frac{1}{2}b = c$, so $\frac{c}{b} = \frac{1}{2}$

$4c = 3d$, so $\frac{d}{c} = \frac{1}{2}$

Now substitute these values into the equation above:

$$\frac{d}{a} = \frac{b}{a} \times \frac{c}{b} \times \frac{d}{c}$$

$$= \frac{1}{2} \times \frac{1}{2} \times \frac{4}{3}$$

$$= \frac{4}{12} = \frac{1}{3}$$

Method III:

And, if all of this algebra confuses you, you can also solve this problem by picking a value for a. Then, by using the relationship given, determine what value d must have and hence the value of $\frac{d}{a}$.

Since terms have coefficients of 2, 3, and 4, it's best to pick a number that's a multiple of 2, 3, and 4. Then we're less likely to have to deal with calculations involving fractions. Say a is 12. Since $a = 2b$, then $b = 6$. Since $\frac{1}{2}b = c$, then $c = 3$. Finally, if $4c = 3d$, we get $4 \times 3 = 3d$, or $d = 4$. Then the ratio of d to a is $\frac{4}{12}$, or $\frac{1}{3}$.

28. In each case the examination and the frames are the same; the difference in cost must be due to a difference in the costs of the lenses. Since plastic lenses cost four times as much as glass lenses, the difference in cost must be three times the cost of the glass lenses.

$$\text{Difference in cost} = \text{Cost of plastic} - \text{Cost of glass}$$
$$s = 4\,(\text{cost of glass}) - 1\,(\text{cost of glass})$$
$$= 3\,(\text{cost of glass})$$

The difference in cost is $42 - 30$, or $12. Since this is 3 times the cost of the glass lenses, the glass lenses must cost, $\dfrac{\$12}{3}$ or $4.

29. In this question we cannot determine the number of white mice or gray mice, but we can still determine their ratio.

Since $\dfrac{1}{2}$ of the white mice make up $\dfrac{1}{8}$ of the total mice, the **total** number of white mice must be double $\dfrac{1}{8}$ of the total number of mice, or $\dfrac{1}{4}$ of the total number of mice. Algebraically, if $\dfrac{1}{2} \times W = \dfrac{1}{8} \times T$, then $W = \dfrac{1}{4} \times T$. So $\dfrac{1}{4}$ of the total mice are white. Similarly, since $\dfrac{1}{3}$ of the number of gray mice is $\dfrac{1}{9}$ of the total number of mice $3 \times \dfrac{1}{9}$ of all the mice, or $\dfrac{1}{3}$ of all the mice are gray mice. Therefore, the ratio of white mice to gray mice is $\dfrac{1}{4}:\dfrac{1}{3}$, which is the same as $\dfrac{3}{12}:\dfrac{4}{12}$, or 3:4.

30. One of the two integers is odd and the other is even. If two numbers have an even product, at least one of the numbers is even, so we can eliminate choice (A).

    If both numbers were even, their sum would be even, but we know the sum of these numbers is odd, so we can eliminate choice (B). If one number is odd and the other is even, their product is even and their sum is odd. Choice (C) gives us what we're looking for. Choices (D) and (E) both can be true, but they're not necessarily true.

31. Since these four integers have an even product, at least one of them must be even, so Roman numeral I, 0, is impossible. Is it possible for exactly 2 of the 4 to be even? If there are 2 odds and 2 evens, the sum is even, since odd + odd = even and even + even = even. Also, if there's at least 1 even among the integers, the product is even, so roman numeral II is possible. Similarly, roman numeral III gives an even product and even sum, so our answer is II and III only.

32. The wire can be divided into three equal parts, each with integral length, so the minimum length must be a multiple of 3. Unfortunately, all of the answer choices are multiples of 3. One of those 3 pieces is cut into 8 pieces, again all with integer lengths, so the length of the wire must be at least $3 \cdot 8$ or 24. Another of those three segments is cut into 6 pieces. Now, what does that mean? Each third can be divided into either 6 or 8 segments with integer lengths. In other words, the thirds have an integer length evenly divisible by both 6 and 8. The least common multiple of 6 and 8 is 24, so the minimum length of the wire is $3 \cdot 24$ or 72.

33. Here we want to determine, basically, how many numbers between 0 and 60 are even multiples of 5. Well, all even multiples of 5 must be multiples of 10. So, the multiples of 10 between 0 and 60 are 10, 20, 30, 40, and 50. That's 5 altogether.

34. The average of a group of evenly spaced numbers is equal to the middle number. Here there is an even number of terms (18), so the average is between the two middle numbers, the 9th and 10th terms. This tells us that the 9th consecutive odd integer here will be the first odd integer less than 534, which is 533. Once we have the 9th term, we can count backward to find the first.

    10th: 535

    Average: 534

    9th: 533

    8th: 531

    7th: 529

    6th: 527

    5th: 525

    4th: 523

    3rd: 521

    2nd: 519

    1st: 517

35. This is a good opportunity to use the "balance" method. We're told the average closing price for all five days: $75.50. We're also given the closing prices for the first four days. Using the "balance" method we make the fifth day "balance out" the first four:

Monday	$75.58	average + $0.08
Tuesday	$75.63	average + $0.13
Wednesday	$75.42	average + $0.08
Thursday	$75.52	average + $0.02
after four days		average + $0.15

    To make the values "balance out" the fifth day must be (average − $0.15) or $75.35.

36. We can't find individual values for any of these six numbers. However, with the given information we can find the sum of the six numbers, and the sum of just the largest and smallest. Subtracting the sum of the smallest and largest from the sum of all six will leave us with the sum of the four others, from which we can find *their* average.

    The sum of all six numbers is (average of all 6 numbers) × (number of values) = 5 × 6, or 30.

    The sum of the greatest and smallest can be found in the same way: 2 × average = 2 × 7 = 14. The sum of the other four numbers is (the sum of all six) − (the sum of the greatest and smallest) = (30 − 14) = 16.

    The sum of the other four numbers is 16. Their average is $\frac{16}{4}$ or 4.

37. The key to doing this problem is to link what we're given to what we need to find. We need to solve for the average of $a + 3$, $b - 5$, and 6. If we could determine their sum, then all we'd need to do is divide this sum by 3 to find their average.

    Well, we don't know a and b, but we can determine their sum. We are given the average of a, b and 7. Clearly we can figure out the sum of these 3 values by multiplying the average by the number of terms. 13 times 3 = 39. That allows us to determine the sum of a and b. If $a + b + 7 = 39$, then $a + b = 39 - 7$, or 32.

    Now, remember we're asked for the average of $a + 3$, $b - 5$ and 6. The sum of these expressions can be rewritten as $a + b + 3 - 5 + 6$, or, as $a + b + 4$. If $a + b = 32$, then $a + b + 4 = 32 + 4$, or 36. Therefore, the sum is 36 and the number of terms is 3, so the average is $\frac{36}{3}$, or 12.

CHAPTER TWO

Algebra

The algebra tested on the GRE is of the straightforward high school variety: evaluate an expression, solve an equation or inequality, etc. But that doesn't mean you should take it lightly. If you're out of practice, be sure to review. The questions here offer a good opportunity for you to gauge your skills.

EQUATIONS & EXPRESSIONS

1. If $4x^2 - 7xy + 3y^2 = 7$ and $8y^2 + 9x^2 - 7xy = 22$, what is the value of $x^2 + y^2$?

   (A) 0
   (B) 2
   (C) 3 ✓
   (D) 7
   (E) It cannot be determined from the information given.

   [handwritten:] $9x^2 - 7xy + 8y^2 = 22$
   $+ \ 4x^2 - 7xy + 3y^2 = 7$
   $5x^2 - 14xy \ 5y^2 = 15$

   $5x^2 + 5y^2 = 15$
   $5(x^2 + y^2) = 15$
   $x^2 + y^2 = 3$

2. If $y > 0$, $4x = 2y^2 + 2z$, and $z - 4 = 11y^2$, what is y in terms of x?

   (A) $\sqrt{\dfrac{7-x}{6}}$

   (B) $\sqrt{\dfrac{x}{6}}$

   (C) $\sqrt{\dfrac{7+x}{6}}$

   (D) $\sqrt{\dfrac{x-7}{6}}$

   (E) $\sqrt{\dfrac{x+7}{6}}$

   [handwritten:] $z = 11y^2 + 4$
   $4x = 2y^2 + 2(11y^2 + 4)$
   $4x = 2y^2 + 22y^2 + 8$
   $4x = 24y^2 + 8$
   $x = 6y^2 + 2$
   $\sqrt{\dfrac{x-2}{6}} = y$

3. If $x = \dfrac{y}{7}, \dfrac{y}{r} = \dfrac{x}{s}$, and r, s, x, and y are nonzero integers, then $\dfrac{r}{s} =$

   (A) $\dfrac{y}{x}$

   (B) $\dfrac{1}{7}$

   (C) $\dfrac{7}{y}$

   (D) $\dfrac{x}{7}$

   (E) 7 ✓

   [handwritten:] $7x = y$ $sy = rx$
   $y = \dfrac{rx}{s}$
   $7x = \dfrac{rx}{s}$
   $\dfrac{7x}{x} = \dfrac{rx}{s \cdot x}$
   $7 = r/s$

4. If $x = \dfrac{13m^2 + 7m - 4}{16n^2 - 8n + 10} + \dfrac{16n^2 - 8n + 10}{13m^2 + 7m - 4}$ and $y = \dfrac{13m^2 + 7m - 4}{16n^2 - 8n + 10} - \dfrac{16n^2 - 8n + 10}{13m^2 + 7m - 4}$,

   then $y^2 - x^2 =$ *[handwritten:]* $(y+x)(y-x)$

   (A) -4 ✓
   (B) 0
   (C) 2
   (D) $\dfrac{169m^4 + 49m^2 + 16}{256n^2 + 64n + 100p}$
   (E) $\dfrac{256n^2 + 64n + 100}{169m^4 + 49m^2 + 16}$

   [handwritten working:]
   $\dfrac{13m^2 + 7m - 4}{16n^2 - 8n + 10} + \dfrac{16n^2 - 8n + 10}{13m^2 + 7m - 4} + \dfrac{13m^2 + 7m - 4}{16n^2 - 8n + 10} - \dfrac{16n^2 - 8n + 10}{13m^2 + 7m - 4}$

   $\left[2 \left(\dfrac{13m^2 + 7m - 4}{16n^2 - 8n + 10} \right) \right] \cdot \left[-2 \left(\dfrac{16n^2 - 8n + 10}{13m^2 + 7m - 4} \right) \right]$

   -4

5. The equation $256\left(\frac{1}{4}g^4 + \frac{1}{16}g^3 - \frac{1}{32}g^2 + \frac{1}{64}g - \frac{1}{128}\right) = ag^4 + bg^3 + cg^2 + dg + e$ is true for all values of g. If a, b, c, d, and e are constants, then $a + b + c + d + e = ?$
   (A) 74
   (B) 84
   (C) 168
   (D) 244
   (E) 256

FUNCTIONS & SYMBOLS

6. If $k(x) = 2x^4 + 6x^2 + 7$, what is the smallest possible value of $k(x)$?
   (A) 0
   (B) 2
   (C) 6
   (D) 7
   (E) 15

7. If $[a] = \dfrac{6a^2 - 3a + 7}{2}$ for all integers a and $b = [1]$, then $[b] - b =$
   (A) 43
   (B) 57
   (C) 66
   (D) 71
   (E) 80

8. If ¥f is defined as the sum of all the positive odd integers between 0 and f for all positive even values of f such that ¥6 = 1 + 3 + 5 = 9, which of the following is equivalent to ¥20?
   (A) ¥10 + ¥10
   (B) ¥2 × ¥10
   (C) ¥10 + ¥12 + ¥14
   (D) ¥2 + ¥6 + ¥10 + ¥16
   (E) ¥2 + ¥6 + ¥8 + ¥10 + ¥14

9. Let ♪r be defined as $-6r^2 + 14r + 4$. If ♪r = ♪$(r + 3)$, what is the value of r?
   (A) $-\dfrac{1}{2}$
   (B) $-\dfrac{1}{3}$
   (C) 0
   (D) $\dfrac{1}{4}$
   (E) $\dfrac{1}{2}$

10. If $x(a) = \sqrt[3]{3a^2 + 5a - 16}$, $y(b) = \sqrt{12b - 8}$, and $z(c) = 2c + 2$, then what is the value of $x(y(z(2)))$ when a, b, and c are positive?

    (A) 4
    (B) 5
    (C) 6
    (D) 7
    (E) 8

EXPONENTS & INEQUALITIES

11. $4^c + 4^{c+1} + 4^{c+2} =$

    (A) 12^c
    (B) 12^{3c+3}
    (C) $21^c - 3$
    (D) $4(21^c)$
    (E) $21(4^c)$

12. If the integers a, b, and c are either all positive or all negative, $a < b < c$, and $|a + b + c| < 10$, how many possible values are there for c?

    (A) Two
    (B) Four
    (C) Six
    (D) Eight
    (E) Ten

13. If $81^{y+2} = (y + 1)^{16}$, then $y =$

    (A) 0
    (B) 1
    (C) 2
    (D) 4
    (E) 5

14. If m is an integer and $m! < 1,000$ and $(m - 2)! > 10$, then $m! - (m - 2)! =$

    (A) 5
    (B) 22
    (C) 114
    (D) 327
    (E) 696

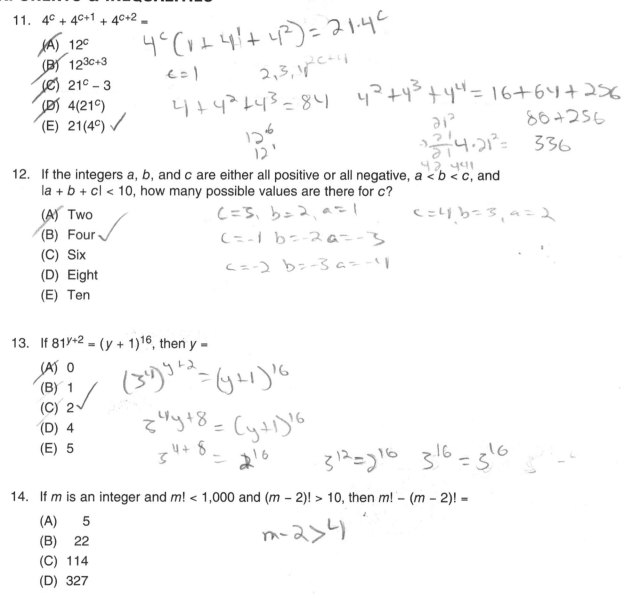

15. If x is an integer and $\dfrac{x^2 - 5x + 6}{x - 2} < 0$, which of the following represents all values of x?

    (A) $x < -3$
    (B) $x < -2$
    (C) $x < 2$
    (D) $x < 3$
    (E) $x < 6$

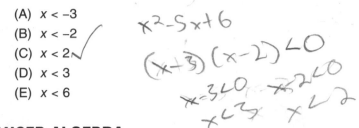

ADVANCED ALGEBRA

16. If $abc \neq 0$, then $\dfrac{a^2bc + ab^2c + abc^2}{abc} =$

    (A) $a + b + c$
    (B) $\dfrac{a + b + c}{abc}$
    (C) $a^3b^3c^3$
    (D) $3abc$
    (E) $2abc$

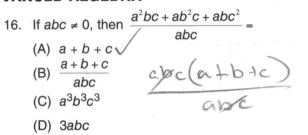

17. The expression $\dfrac{3}{x - 1} - 6$ will equal 0 when x equals which of the following?

    (A) -3
    (B) $-\dfrac{2}{3}$
    (C) $\dfrac{1}{2}$
    (D) $\dfrac{3}{2}$
    (E) 3

18. If $x > 1$ and $\dfrac{a}{b} = 1 - \dfrac{1}{x}$, then $\dfrac{b}{a} =$

    (A) x
    (B) $x - 1$
    (C) $\dfrac{x - 1}{x}$
    (D) $\dfrac{x}{x - 1}$
    (E) $\dfrac{1}{x} - 1$

19. If $m \blacktriangle n$ is defined by the equation $m \blacktriangle n = \dfrac{m^2 - n + 1}{mn}$, for all nonzero m and n, then $3 \blacktriangle 1 =$

    (A) $\dfrac{9}{4}$
    (B) 3
    (C) $\dfrac{11}{3}$
    (D) 6
    (E) 9

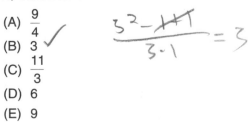

20. If $y > 0$ and $3y - 2 = \dfrac{-1}{3y + 2}$, then $y =$

    (A) $\dfrac{1}{3}$

    (B) $\dfrac{\sqrt{3}}{3}$

    (C) 1

    (D) $\sqrt{3}$

    (E) $\sqrt{3} + 1$

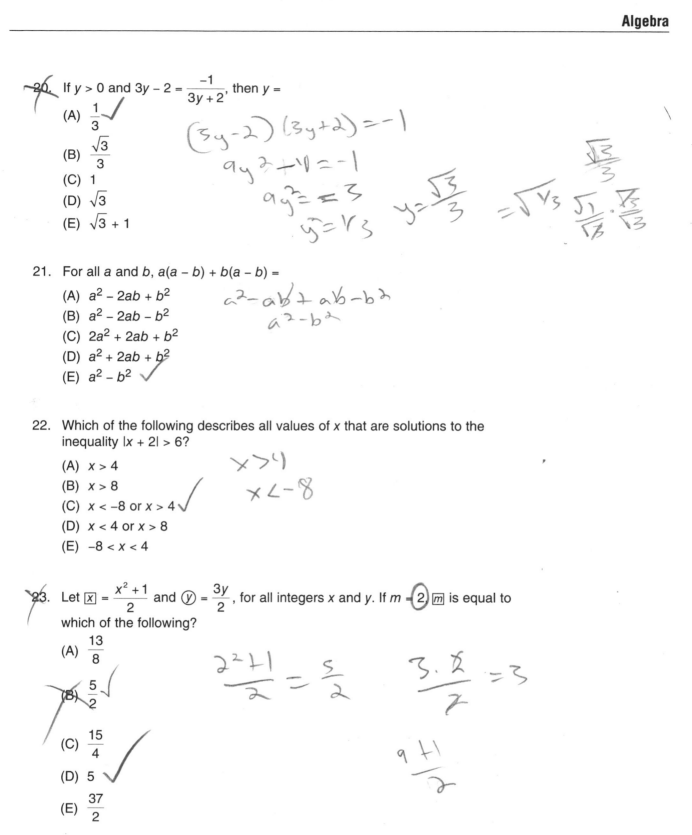

21. For all a and b, $a(a - b) + b(a - b) =$

    (A) $a^2 - 2ab + b^2$

    (B) $a^2 - 2ab - b^2$

    (C) $2a^2 + 2ab + b^2$

    (D) $a^2 + 2ab + b^2$

    (E) $a^2 - b^2$

22. Which of the following describes all values of x that are solutions to the inequality $|x + 2| > 6$?

    (A) $x > 4$

    (B) $x > 8$

    (C) $x < -8$ or $x > 4$

    (D) $x < 4$ or $x > 8$

    (E) $-8 < x < 4$

23. Let $\boxed{x} = \dfrac{x^2 + 1}{2}$ and $\textcircled{y} = \dfrac{3y}{2}$, for all integers x and y. If $m = 2$, $\boxed{m}$ is equal to which of the following?

    (A) $\dfrac{13}{8}$

    (B) $\dfrac{5}{2}$

    (C) $\dfrac{15}{4}$

    (D) 5

    (E) $\dfrac{37}{2}$

24. If $x^2 - 9 < 0$, which of the following is true?

    (A) $x < -3$ ✓
    (B) $x > 3$
    (C) $x > 9$
    (D) $x < -3$ or $x > 3$
    (E) $-3 < x < 3$

    (handwritten) $(x-3)(x+3) < 0$

    $x - 3 < 0 \quad x+3 < 0$

    $x < 3 \quad x < -3$

25. If $n > 4$, which of the following is equivalent to $\dfrac{n - 4\sqrt{n} + 4}{\sqrt{n} - 2}$?

    (A) $\sqrt{n}$
    (B) $2\sqrt{n}$
    (C) $\sqrt{n} + 2$
    (D) $\sqrt{n} - 2$ ✓
    (E) $n + \sqrt{n}$

    (handwritten) $n = 9$

    $\dfrac{9 - 4\sqrt{9} + 4}{\sqrt{9} - 2}$

    $\dfrac{9 - 4\cdot 3 + 4}{3 - 2} = 9 - 12 + 4$

    $\dfrac{16 - 4\sqrt{4} + 4}{4 - 2} = 24 - 2 = 2$

26. What is the set of all values of x for which $x^2 - 3x - 18 = 0$?

    (A) $\{-6\}$
    (B) $\{-3\}$
    (C) $\{-3, 6\}$ ✓
    (D) $\{3, 6\}$
    (E) $\{2, 6\}$

    (handwritten) $x^2 - 3x - 18$

    $(x - 6)(x + 3)$

    $x = 6 \quad x = -3$

ALGEBRA PRACTICE SET ANSWER KEY

1.	C	14.	E
2.	D	15.	C
3.	E	16.	A
4.	A	17.	D
5.	A	18.	D
6.	D	19.	B
7.	C	20.	B
8.	E	21.	E
9.	B	22.	C
10.	C	23.	D
11.	E	24.	E
12.	C	25.	D
13.	C	26.	C

EXPLANATIONS

1. When the GRE asks for the value of $x^2 + y^2$, you usually won't be able to determine the value of either x^2 or y^2 alone. Rewrite the second equation as $9x^2 - 7xy + 8y^2 = 22$, then use combination to solve the system of equations:

$$\begin{array}{r} 9x^2 - 7xy + 8y^2 = 22 \\ -(4x^2 - 7xy + 3y^2 = 7) \\ \hline 5x^2 + 5y^2 = 15 \\ 5(x^2 + y^2) = 15 \\ x^2 + y^2 = 3 \end{array}$$

2. You'll need to get rid of z before you can solve for y in terms of x, so add 5 to both sides of the equation $z - 4 = 11y^2$ to get $z = 11y^2 + 4$. Now plug this in for z in the first equation and solve for y:

$$4x = 2y^2 + 2z$$
$$4x = 2y^2 + 2(11y^2 + 4)$$
$$4x = 2y^2 + 22y^2 + 28$$
$$4x = 24y^2 + 28$$
$$x = 6y^2 + 7$$
$$6y^2 = x - 7$$
$$y^2 = \frac{x-7}{6}$$
$$y = \sqrt{\frac{x-7}{6}}$$

3. With so many variables present, you may have been tempted to pick numbers, but a bit of critical thinking can make this problem much easier. If you divide $x = \frac{y}{7}$ by s on both sides, you'll have $\frac{x}{s} = \frac{y}{7s}$. Since $\frac{y}{r} = \frac{x}{s}$, $7s = r$ and $\frac{r}{s} = 7$.

4. The problem looks hideous, and the mere thought of the algebra required to figure this out is enough to make many a GRE test taker feel lightheaded. As an advanced test taker, remember that overly complex constructions on the GRE are the test maker's way of saying, "Look for an easier way." In this case, noticing that the two ugly expressions Look *very* similar and remembering that $y^2 - x^2 = (y - x)(y + x)$ will allow you to avoid a lot of really ugly algebra:

$$y^2 - x^2 = (y - x)(y + x)$$

$$= \left[\left(\frac{13m^2 + 7m - 4}{16n^2 - 8n + 10} - \frac{16n^2 - 8n + 10}{13m^2 + 7m - 4} \right) - \left(\frac{13m^2 + 7m - 4}{16n^2 - 8n + 10} + \frac{16n^2 - 8n + 10}{13m^2 + 7m - 4} \right) \right]$$

$$\left[\left(\frac{13m^2 + 7m - 4}{16n^2 - 8n + 10} - \frac{16n^2 - 8n + 10}{13m^2 + 7m - 4} \right) + \left(\frac{13m^2 + 7m - 4}{16n^2 - 8n + 10} + \frac{16n^2 - 8n + 10}{13m^2 + 7m - 4} \right) \right]$$

$$= \left[-2 \left(\frac{16n^2 - 8n + 10}{13m^2 + 7m - 4} \right) \right] \left[2 \left(\frac{13m^2 + 7m - 4}{16n^2 - 8n + 10} \right) \right]$$

$$= -2(2)$$

$$= -4$$

5. Begin by simplifying the left side of the equation:

$$256\left(\frac{1}{4}g^4 + \frac{1}{16}g^3 - \frac{1}{32}g^2 + \frac{1}{64}g - \frac{1}{128}\right) = 64g^4 + 16g^3 - 8g^2 + 4g - 2e$$

For $ag^4 + bg^3 + cg^2 + dg + e$ to be true for *all* values of g, the coefficients 64, 16, −8, 4, and −2 must equal a, b, c, d, and e, respectively. That means $a + b + c + d + e = 64 + 16 - 8 + 4 - 2 = 74$.

6. The smallest possible value of $k(x)$ comes from the smallest possible value for x. Since the variable terms have positive even powers, neither can be negative, so the smallest possible value for $2x^4$ and $6x^2$ is at $x = 0$. If $x = 0$, $2x^4 + 6x^2 + 7 = 7$, which is choice (D).

7. There's a lot going on here, so take things one step at a time to avoid getting overwhelmed. You are told that $b = [1]$, so begin by plugging 1 for a into the defining equation:

$$[1] = \frac{6(1)^2 - 3(1) + 7}{2} = \frac{6 - 3 + 7}{2} = \frac{10}{2} = 5$$

Now plug 5 into the defining equation to find $[b]$:

$$[5] = \frac{6(5)^2 - 3(5) + 7}{2} = \frac{6(25) - 15 + 7}{2} = \frac{150 - 15 + 7}{2} = \frac{142}{2} = 71$$

So $b = 5$ and $[b] = 71$, and their difference is $71 - 5 = 66$.

8. The strange symbol may spook some, but an advanced test taker like yourself should recognize this as a plug-and-chug much like any other algebra problem with variables. To find the expression equivalent to ¥20, first evaluate ¥20: ¥20 = 1 + 3 + 5 + 7 + 9 + 11 + 13 + 15 + 17 + 19 = 100. Now evaluate the choices to see which comes out to 100 (if you noticed that $¥f = \left(\frac{f}{2}\right)^2$, the choices become much quicker to evaluate):

(A) $(1 + 3 + 5 + 7 + 9) + (1 + 3 + 5 + 7 + 9) = 25 + 25 = 50 \neq 100$. Eliminate.

(B) $(1) \times (1 + 3 + 5 + 7 + 9) = 25 \neq 100$. Eliminate.

(C) $(1 + 3 + 5 + 7 + 9) + (1 + 3 + 5 + 7 + 9 + 11) + (1 + 3 + 5 + 7 + 9 + 11 + 13) = 25 + 36 + 49 = 110 \neq 100$. Eliminate.

(D) $(1) + (1 + 3 + 5) + (1 + 3 + 5 + 7 + 9) + (1 + 3 + 5 + 7 + 9 + 11 + 13 + 15) = 1 + 9 + 25 + 64 = 99 \neq 100$. Eliminate.

(E) $(1) + (1 + 3 + 5) + (1 + 3 + 5 + 7) + (1 + 3 + 5 + 7 + 9) + (1 + 3 + 5 + 7 + 9 + 11 + 13) = 1 + 9 + 16 + 25 + 49 = 100$. This works.

Only (E) works, so it must be correct.

9. The problem defines a function, so evaluate the equation using that definition:

$$♪r = ♪(r + 3)$$

$$-6r^2 + 14r + 4 = -6(r + 3)^2 + 14(r + 3) + 4$$

$$-6r^2 + 14r + 4 = -6(r^2 + 6r + 9) + 14r + 42 + 4$$

$$-6r^2 + 14r + 4 = -6r^2 - 36r - 54 + 14r + 42 + 4$$

$$-6r^2 + 14r + 4 = -6r^2 - 22r - 8$$

$$36r = -12$$

$$r = -\frac{12}{36} = -\frac{1}{3}$$

10. With nested functions, remember to work inside out:

$$z(2) = 2(2) + 2 = 4 + 2 = 6$$

$$y(6) = \sqrt{12(6) - 8} = \sqrt{72 - 8} = \sqrt{64} = 8$$

$$x(8) = \sqrt[3]{3(8)^2 + 5(8) - 16} = \sqrt[3]{3(64) + 40 - 16} = \sqrt[3]{192 + 24} = \sqrt[3]{216} = 6$$

11. The key to simplifying this equation algebraically is to factor out a 4^c:

$$4^c + 4^{c+1} + 4^{c+2} = 4^c(4^0 + 4^1 + 4^2) = 4^c(1 + 4 + 16) = (21)4^c$$

You could also pick numbers. If $c = 0$, then $4^c + 4^{c+1} + 4^{c+2} = 4^0 + 4^1 + 4^2 = (1 + 4 + 16) = 21$.

Now test $c = 0$ in each of the choices:

(A) $12^0 = 1 \neq 21$. Eliminate.
(B) $12^{3(0)+3} = 12^3 \neq 21$. Eliminate.
(C) $21^0 - 3 = 1 - 3 = -2 \neq 21$. Eliminate.
(D) $4(21^0) = 4(1) = 4 \neq 21$. Eliminate.
(E) $21(4^0) = 21(1) = 21$. This works.

12. When the GRE combines absolute value with inequalities, remember that $-1 > -2$. If a, b, and c are positive, $a = 1$ and $b = 2$ would allow c to be any of 3, 4, 5, or 6. If a, b, and c are negative, c can be -1 or -2 (a c value of -3 or less would result in a minimum value of $|(-5) + (-4) + (-3)| = 12$ for $|a + b + c|$). That's a total of six values for c.

13. This problem can be an absolute nightmare to take head on, but an advanced test taker such as yourself knows to look for a shortcut when the GRE presents you with a seemingly impossible problem. While your first instinct may have been to back-solve, it is actually much easier with elimination! (See the chapter on word problems for a further explanation of the back-solving and elimination strategies.) The key here is that y is an integer (since all

five choices are integers), so $y + 1$ *must* be a factor of 81. Of the choices, only (A) and (C) produce factors of 81. Choice (A) doesn't work, as $1^{16} = 1$, so (C) must be correct.

To see the math, back-solve (C):

(C) $81^{2+2} = (2 + 1)^{16}$

$$81^4 = 3^{16}$$

$$(3^4)^4 = 3^{16}$$

$$3^{16} = 3^{16}$$

14. The "!" symbol represents a factorial, and $m!$ is defined as $m \times (m - 1) \times (m - 2) \times \ldots \times 1$. If m is an integer and $m!$ is less than 1,000, then m is at most 6, as $6! = 6 \times 5 \times 4 \times 3 \times 2 \times 1 = 720$ and $7! = 7 \times 6 \times 5 \times 4 \times 3 \times 2 \times 1 = 5,040$. If $(m - 2)!$ is greater than 10, then $m - 2$ must be greater than 3, as $3 \times 2 \times 1 = 6$. Since m is no larger than 6 and $m - 2$ *is* larger than 3, m must be 6.

$$6! - (6 - 2)! = 6! - 4! = (6 \times 5 \times 4 \times 3 \times 2 \times 1) - (4 \times 3 \times 2 \times 1) = 720 - 24 = 696$$

15. $\dfrac{x^2 - 5x + 6}{x - 2} = \dfrac{(x-2)(x-3)}{x-2} = x - 3$, so $x - 3 < 0$ and $x < 3$. Be careful not to fall into the trap at the last minute! x can't be 2 either or else the denominator of the original fraction, $x - 2$, would be undefined. Since x is an integer less than 3 and x can't be 2, $x < 2$ is correct.

16. In this problem, the expression has three terms in the numerator, and a single term, abc, in the denominator. Since the three terms in the numerator each have abc as a factor, abc can be factored out from both the numerator and the denominator, and the expression can be reduced to a simpler form.

$$\frac{a^2 bc + ab^2 c + abc^2}{abc}$$

$$= \frac{a(abc) + b(abc) + c(abc)}{abc}$$

$$= \frac{(a + b + c)(abc)}{abc}$$

$$= (a + b + c) \cdot \frac{abc}{abc}$$

$$= a + b + c$$

17. We are asked to find x when $\dfrac{3}{x-1} - 6 = 0$. Clear the denominator by multiplying both sides by $x - 1$.

$$\frac{3}{x-1}(x-1) - 6(x-1) = 0(x-1)$$

$3 - 6(x-1) = 0$ Remove parentheses.

$3 - 6x + 6 = 0$ Gather like terms.

$9 - 6x = 0$ Isolate the variable.

$9 - 6x + 6x = 0 + 6x$

$9 = 6x$

$$\frac{9}{6} = \frac{6x}{6}$$

$$\frac{3}{2} = x$$

Answer choice (D) is correct. You can check your answer by plugging $\dfrac{3}{2}$ into the original equation:

$$\frac{3}{\dfrac{3}{2} - 1} - 6 = \frac{3}{\dfrac{1}{2}} - 6 = 6 - 6 = 0$$

18. Since $\dfrac{b}{a}$ is the reciprocal of $\dfrac{a}{b}$, $\dfrac{b}{a}$ must be the reciprocal of $1 - \dfrac{1}{x}$ as well. Combine the terms in $1 - \dfrac{1}{x}$ and then find the reciprocal.

$$\frac{a}{b} = 1 - \frac{1}{x} = \frac{x}{x} - \frac{1}{x} = \frac{x-1}{x}$$

Therefore, $\dfrac{b}{a} = \dfrac{x}{x-1}$.

19. Here we have a symbolism problem, involving a symbol (▲) that doesn't really exist in mathematics. All you need to do is simply follow the directions given in the definition of this symbol. To find the value of 3 ▲ 1, simply plug 3 and 1 into the formula given for m ▲ n, substituting 3 for m and 1 for n. Then the equation becomes:

$$3 \ ▲ \ 1 = \frac{(3)^2 - (1) + 1}{(3)(1)}$$

$$= \frac{9 - 1 + 1}{3}$$

$$= \frac{9}{3}$$

$$= 3$$

20. First clear the fraction by multiplying both sides of the equation by $3y + 2$.

$$(3y + 2)(3y - 2) = \frac{-1}{(3y + 2)} \cdot (3y + 2)$$

$$9y^2 - 6y + 6y - 4 = -1 \qquad \text{Using FOIL.}$$

$$9y^2 - 4 = -1 \qquad \text{Gathering terms.}$$

$$9y^2 - 4 + 4 = -1 + 4 \qquad \text{Isolating the variable.}$$

$$9y^2 = 3$$

$$y^2 = \frac{3}{9}$$

$$y = \sqrt{\frac{3}{9}}$$

$$y = \frac{\sqrt{3}}{\sqrt{9}}$$

$$y = \frac{\sqrt{3}}{3}$$

(Since $y > 0$, y cannot also equal $-\frac{\sqrt{3}}{3}$.)

21. Here we multiply out the part on each side of the addition sign, then combine like terms. We use the distributive law:

$$a(a - b) + b(a - b) = (a^2 - ab) + (ba - b^2)$$
$$= a^2 - ab + ab - b^2$$
$$= a^2 - b^2$$

Alternatively, we can factor out the common term $(a - b)$, and we're left with a product which is the difference of two perfect squares:

$$a(a - b) + b(a - b) = (a - b)(a + b)$$
$$= a^2 - b^2$$

22. We can think of the absolute value of a number as the number's distance from zero along the number line. Here, since the absolute value of the expression is greater than 6, it could be either that the expression $x + 2$ is **greater than 6** (more than six units to the right of zero) or that the expression is **less than –6** (more than six units to the left of zero). Therefore either

$$x + 2 > 6 \quad \text{or} \quad x + 2 < -6$$
$$x > 4 \quad \text{or} \quad x < -8$$

23. This is an especially tricky symbolism problem. We're given **two** new symbols, and we need to complete several steps. The trick is figuring out where to start. We are asked to find $\boxed{m}$. In order to do this we must first find the value of m. Since m is equal to ②, we can find m by finding the value of ②. And we can find ② by substituting 2 for y in the equation given for ⓨ. The equation becomes:

$$② = \frac{3(2)}{2}$$
$$② = 3$$

Since $m = ②$, then m is equal to 3, and $\boxed{m}$ is just $\boxed{3}$. We find $\boxed{3}$ by substituting 3 for x in the equation given for $\boxed{x}$:

$$\boxed{3} = \frac{3^2 + 1}{2}$$
$$= \frac{9 + 1}{2}$$
$$= \frac{10}{2}$$
$$= 5$$

So $\boxed{m} = 5$.

24. Rearrange $x^2 - 9 < 0$ to get $x^2 < 9$. We're looking for all the values of x that would fit this inequality.

    We need to be very careful and consider both positive **and** negative values of x. Remember that $3^2 = 9$ and also that $(-3)^2 = 9$.

    We can consider the case that x is positive. If x is positive, and $x^2 < 9$, then we can simply say that $x < 3$. But what if x is negative? x can only take on values whose square is less than 9. In other words, x cannot be less than or equal to -3. (Think of smaller numbers like -4 or -5; their squares are greater than 9.)

    So if x is negative, $x > -3$. Since x can also be 0, we can simply write $-3 < x < 3$.

25. We must try to get rid of the denominator by factoring it out of the numerator. $n - 4\sqrt{n} + 4$ is a difficult expression to work with. It may be easier if we let $t = \sqrt{n}$. Keep in mind then that $t^2 = (\sqrt{n})(\sqrt{n}) = n$.

    Then $\quad n - 4\sqrt{n} + 4 = t^2 - 4t + 4$

    Using FOIL in reverse $\quad = (t - 2)(t - 2)$

    $$= (\sqrt{n} - 2)(\sqrt{n} - 2)$$

    So $\quad \dfrac{n - 4\sqrt{n} + 4}{\sqrt{n} - 2} = \dfrac{(\sqrt{n} - 2)(\sqrt{n} - 2)}{(\sqrt{n} - 2)}$

    $$= \sqrt{n} - 2$$

    Or pick a number for n and try each answer choice.

26. Factor the quadratic:

    $$x^2 - 3x - 18 = (x + a)(x + b)$$

    The product of a and b is: $\qquad ab = -18$

    The sum of a and b is: $\qquad a + b = -3$

Try the factors of -18 that add to -3:

Try $a = 3$ $b = -6$: $3 \times (-6) = -18$

$3 + (-6) = -3$

So $x^2 - 3x - 18 = (x + 3)(x - 6) = 0$

If this is zero, either $x + 3 = 0$ i.e., $x = -3$

or $x - 6 = 0$ i.e., $x = 6$

The set of values is therefore $\{-3, 6\}$

CHAPTER THREE

Geometry

As with the other math topics, GRE geometry draws from your high school days. It's a sampling of angles, triangles, rectangles, circles, and the (x, y) coordinate plane. This is true for both the straight math problems and—as you'll soon see—the word problems.

The defining feature of GRE geometry problems, to the extent they can be said to have one, is that they tend to combine different topics in the same question. That is, you will rarely get a question testing only a triangle or only a rectangle. More common is a question that tests your ability with both.

ANGLES & TRIANGLES

1. In the figure below, the dotted line is parallel to the base of the triangle. What is the value of *v*?

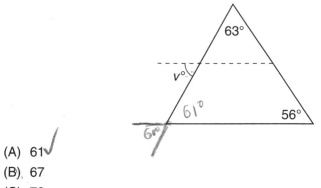

(A) 61 ✓
(B) 67
(C) 72
(D) 74
(E) 77

2. Two parallel lines are cut by a transversal, forming eight angles—*l*, *m*, *n*, *o*, *p*, *q*, *r*, and *s*. If *n*, *q*, *r*, and *s* are acute angles and *l* and *m* are supplementary, which of the following statements must be true?

    I. *o* = *p*

    II. *n* is supplementary to *o*

    III. *q* is supplementary to *l*

    (A) I only
    (B) II only
    (C) III only
    (D) I and II only
    (E) II and III only

all obtuse = each other
all acute equal each other

3. In the figure below, if the area of $\triangle ABC$ is 50, what is the length of $\overline{AD}$?

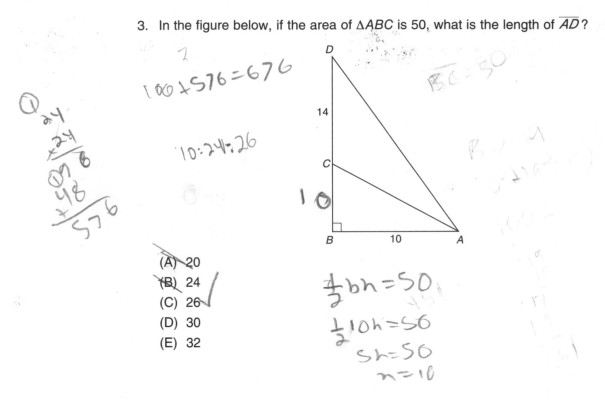

(A) 20
(B) 24
(C) 26
(D) 30
(E) 32

CIRCLES

4. If $\overline{CD}$ is a diameter of the circle below and the closest part of the circle is five feet from the line, what is the value of z?

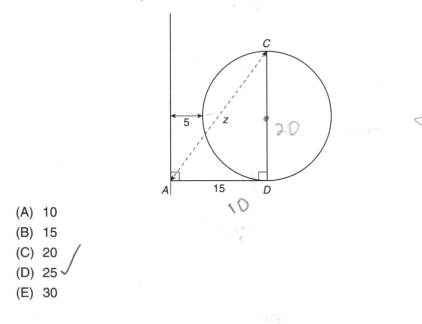

(A) 10
(B) 15
(C) 20
(D) 25
(E) 30

Question 5

5. In the figure below, $\overline{SO}$ is a radius of circle O. What is the length of $\overline{UT}$?

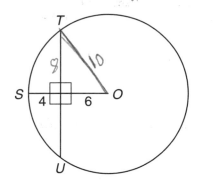

(A) 12

(B) 14

(C) 16

(D) 18

(E) 20

QUADRILATERALS & HEXAGONS

6. In the figure below, $\overline{AB} \parallel \overline{CD}$ and $\overline{AD} \parallel \overline{BC}$. ABCD would have to be a square if which of the following were true?

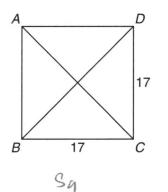

(A) $\overline{BD} \perp \overline{AC}$

(B) $\overline{AB} \cong \overline{DC}$

(C) $\overline{BD} \cong \overline{AC}$

(D) $\overline{AD} \cong \overline{BC}$

(E) $\overline{AB} \cong \overline{AD}$

7. $\overline{XT}$ splits the regular hexagon below into two congruent halves. What is the length of $\overline{XT}$ if one side of the hexagon is 8?

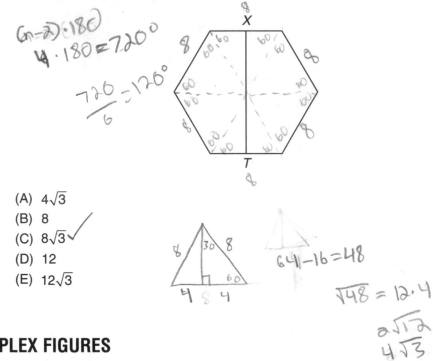

(A) $4\sqrt{3}$
(B) 8
(C) $8\sqrt{3}$ ✓
(D) 12
(E) $12\sqrt{3}$

COMPLEX FIGURES

8. The figure below shows a semicircle attached to a rectangle. If the perimeter of *JKLM* is 74, then the area of *JKLMN* is closest to which of the following?

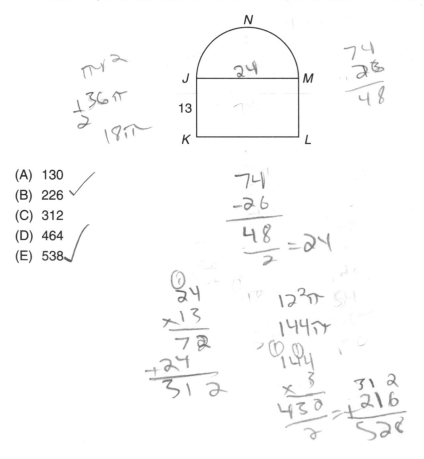

(A) 130
(B) 226 ✓
(C) 312
(D) 464
(E) 538 ✓

9. In the figure below, a circle sits in the middle of four identical squares. What is the area of the shaded region?

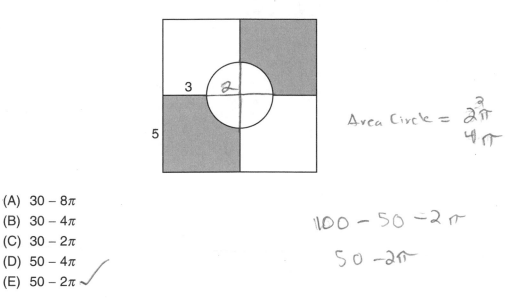

$$\text{Area Circle} = 2\pi^2$$
$$4\pi$$

(A) $30 - 8\pi$

(B) $30 - 4\pi$

(C) $30 - 2\pi$

(D) $50 - 4\pi$

(E) $50 - 2\pi$ ✓

$$100 - 50 - 2\pi$$
$$50 - 2\pi$$

10. In the figure below, three squares lie within a right triangle such that points X, Y, and Z are on the triangle's hypotenuse. What is the value of a?

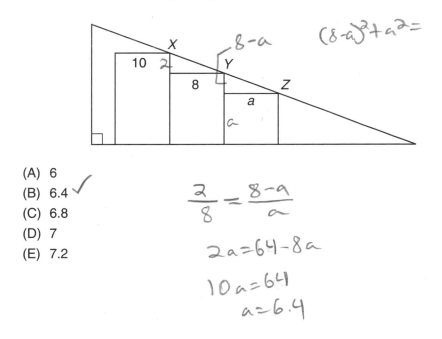

$$(8-a)^2 + a^2 =$$

(A) 6

(B) 6.4 ✓

(C) 6.8

(D) 7

(E) 7.2

$$\frac{2}{8} = \frac{8-a}{a}$$

$$2a = 64 - 8a$$

$$10a = 64$$

$$a = 6.4$$

11. In the figure below, *FGHI* is a square. If $y = 2.5$, what is the area of the unshaded region?

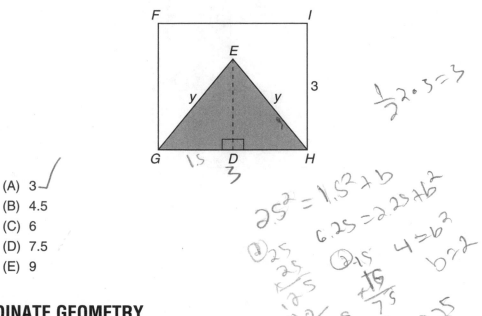

(A) 3

(B) 4.5

(C) 6

(D) 7.5

(E) 9

COORDINATE GEOMETRY

12. The area of circle *G* is 25π. If $\overline{FT}$ is a diameter of circle *G* and *F* corresponds to point (4, 5) on the standard (*x*, *y*) coordinate plane, which one of the following coordinates could be point *T*?

(A) (−6, −5)

(B) (−5, 4)

(C) (−4, 5)

(D) (4, −5)

(E) (6, 5)

13. Two shaded squares and a shaded triangle are shown in the standard (x, y) coordinate plane below with point O as the origin. If the shaded triangle has an area of 5, what is the area of the unshaded region of $ABOCDEF$?

(handwritten on figure: 9, 4, 5, 4, 16, 5, 5, 25, 5, 16, 5)

(0, 9) A
F (4, 9)
(0, 5) B
E (9, 4)
O (5, 0) C   D (9, 0)

(handwritten work: 25 - △   Area = 81   81 - 5 - 32 = 81 - 37   = 44 $\frac{1}{2} \cdot 5 \cdot 5 = \frac{25}{2}$ 44 - 12.5 = 31.5)

(A) 17.5
(B) 25
(C) 31.5 ✓
(D) 44
(E) 51.5

SOLIDS

14. What is the area of $\triangle FGH$, which is inscribed in the cube below?

F   L
J   K
G   M
5
I   H

(handwritten work: $5\sqrt{10} \cdot 5\sqrt{10}$ $5^2 + 5^2\sqrt{10}$ $\frac{1}{2} 25 + 250 \cdot 375$ $5\sqrt{10} \cdot 5\sqrt{10}$ 2510 $125 + 125 = 250$ $25 \cdot 10$ $25\sqrt{2}$ $5\sqrt{10}$ $\frac{1}{2} 5 \cdot 5\sqrt{10}$ $25\sqrt{10}$ $25\sqrt{375}$ $5\sqrt{15}$ $\frac{5\sqrt{10}}{2}$ $5\sqrt{10}$ $5\sqrt{10}$ $\frac{5\sqrt{10}}{2}$)

(A) $5\sqrt{3}$
(B) $5\sqrt{2}$
(C) $\dfrac{25\sqrt{3}}{2}$
(D) $\dfrac{25\sqrt{2}}{2}$ ✓
(E) $25\sqrt{2}$

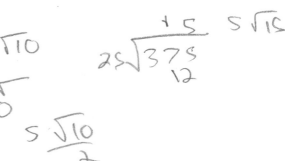

15. The cylindrical can of gravy in the figure below is $\frac{1}{6}$ full. If its contents were poured into an empty can with the same height but half the diameter, how full would the new can be?

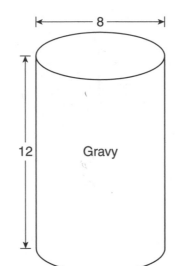

(A) $\frac{1}{4}$

(B) $\frac{1}{3}$

(C) $\frac{1}{2}$

(D) $\frac{2}{3}$ ✓

(E) $\frac{3}{4}$

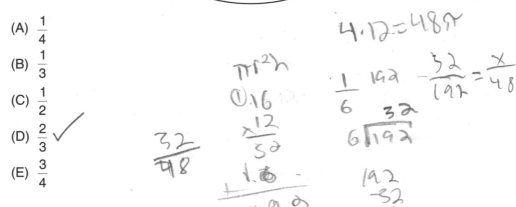

ADVANCED GEOMETRY

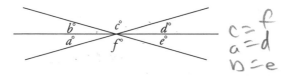

16. Which of the following must be true of the angles marked in the figure above?

    I. $a + b = d + e$ ✓

    II. $b + e = c + f$

    III. $a + c + e = b + d + f$ ✓

(A) I only

(B) I and II only

(C) I and III only ✓

(D) II and III only

(E) I, II, and III

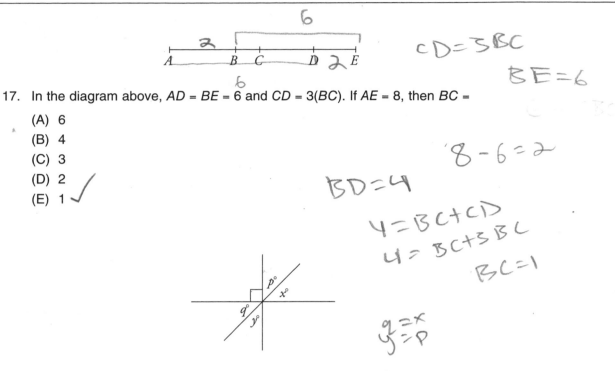

CD = 3BC
BE = 6

17. In the diagram above, $AD = BE = 6$ and $CD = 3(BC)$. If $AE = 8$, then $BC =$

(A) 6
(B) 4
(C) 3
(D) 2
(E) 1 ✓

8 − 6 = 2

BD = 4

$4 = BC + CD$
$4 = BC + 3BC$
$BC = 1$

$q = x$
$y = p$

18. According to the diagram above, which of the following MUST be true?

I. $p = x$ and $q = y$
II. $x + y = 90$
III. $x = y = 45$

(A) I only
(B) II only
(C) III only
(D) I and III only
(E) I, II, and III ✓

$q + y = 90$

$y = p$
$x + y = 90$

$p + x = 90$
$y + ?$

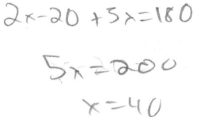

19. In the figure above, $x =$

(A) 40 ✓
(B) 60
(C) 80
(D) 100
(E) 120

$2x − 20 + 5x = 180$

$5x = 200$

$x = 40$

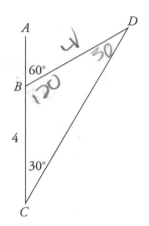

20. In the figure above, if ∠*DBA* has measure 60°, ∠*DCB* has measure 30°, and *BC* = 4, what is the length of *BD*?

    (A) $\sqrt{2}$

    (B) 4

    (C) $4\sqrt{2}$

    (D) $4\sqrt{3}$

    (E) 8

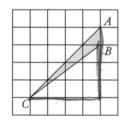

21. The figure consists of 36 squares each with a side of 1. What is the area of △*ABC*?

    (A) 8

    (B) 6

    (C) 4

    (D) 2

    (E) $\dfrac{1}{2}$

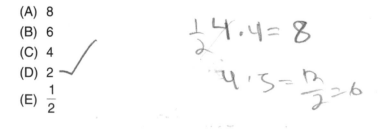

22. The lengths of two sides of a right triangle are $\frac{d}{3}$ and $\frac{d}{4}$, where $d > 0$. If one of these sides is the hypotenuse, what is the length of the third side of the triangle?

    (A) $\frac{5d}{12}$

    (B) $\frac{d}{\sqrt{7}}$

    (C) $\frac{d}{5}$

    (D) $\frac{d}{12}$

    (E) $\frac{d\sqrt{7}}{12}$

23. What is the length in feet of a ladder 24 feet from the foot of a building that reaches up 18 feet along the wall of the building?

    (A) 26
    (B) 28
    (C) 29
    (D) 30
    (E) 32

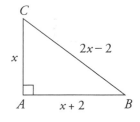

24. In right triangle ABC above, $x =$
    (A) 6
    (B) 8
    (C) $6\sqrt{2}$
    (D) 10
    (E) 13

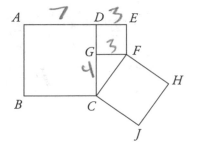

25. In the figure above, square *ABCD* has area 49 and square *DEFG* has area 9. What is the area of square *FCJH*?

    (A) 25
    (B) 32
    (C) 40
    (D) 48
    (E) 69

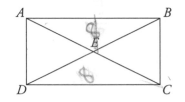

26. In the figure above, *ABCD* is a rectangle. If the area of △*AEB* is 8, what is the area of △*ACD*?

    (A)   8
    (B) 12
    (C) 16
    (D) 24
    (E) 32

27. The perimeter of a rectangle is 6*w*. If one side as length $\frac{w}{2}$, what is the area of the rectangle?

    (A) $\frac{w^2}{4}$

    (B) $\frac{5w^2}{4}$

    (C) $\frac{5w^2}{2}$

    (D) $\frac{11w^2}{4}$

    (E) $\frac{11w^2}{2}$

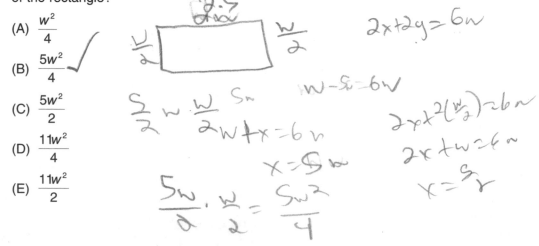

28. The length of each side of square A is increased by 100 percent to make square B. If the length of the side of square B is increased by 50 percent to make square C, by what percent is the area of square C greater than the sum of the areas of squares A and B?

    (A) 75%
    (B) 80%
    (C) 100%
    (D) 150%
    (E) 180%

29. A rectangle with integer side lengths has perimeter 10. What is the greatest number of these rectangles that can be cut from a piece of paper with width 24 and length 60?

    (A) 144
    (B) 180
    (C) 240
    (D) 360
    (E) 480

30. If the diameter of a circle increases by 50 percent, by what percent will the area of the circle increase?

    (A) 25%
    (B) 50%
    (C) 100%
    (D) 125%
    (E) 225%

31. A lighthouse emits a light which can be seen for 60 miles in all directions. If the intensity of the light is strengthened so that its visibility is increased by 40 miles in all directions, by approximately how many square miles is its region of visibility increased?

    (A)   6,300
    (B) 10,000
    (C) 10,300
    (D) 20,000
    (E) 31,400

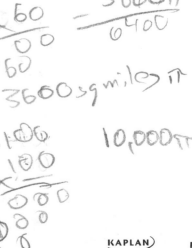

32. If an arc with a length of 12π is $\dfrac{3}{4}$ of the circumference of a circle, what is the shortest distance between the endpoints of the arc?

    (A) 4
    (B) $4\sqrt{2}$
    (C) 8
    (D) $8\sqrt{2}$ ✓
    (E) 16

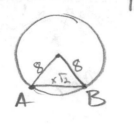

$12\pi = \frac{3}{4}x$

$x = 16\pi$

$C = 16\pi$

$AB_m = 4\pi$

$8\sqrt{2}$

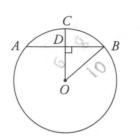

33. In the figure above, O is the center of the circle. If AB has a length of 16 and OB has a length of 10, what is the length of CD?

    (A) 2
    (B) 4 ✓
    (C) $2\sqrt{3}$
    (D) $8 - \sqrt{35}$
    (E) $8 - \sqrt{39}$

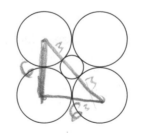

34. The total area of the four equal circles in the figure above is 36π, and the circles are all tangent to one another. What is the diameter of the small circle?

    (A) $6\sqrt{2}$
    (B) $6 + \sqrt{2}$
    (C) $3\sqrt{2} - 3$
    (D) $6\sqrt{2} - 6$ ✓
    (E) $6\sqrt{2} + 6$

9π　　$6\sqrt{2}$

$r = 3$

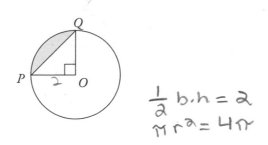

$\frac{1}{2} b \cdot h = 2$

$\pi r^2 = 4\pi$

35. In circle O above, if △POQ is a right triangle and radius OP is 2, what is the area of the shaded region?

$4\pi - 2$

$12 - 2 =$

(A) 4π – 2 ✓

(B) 4π – 4

(C) 2π – 2

(D) 2π – 4

(E) π – 2

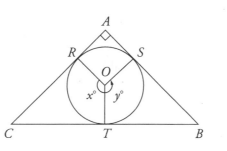

36. In the figure above, right triangle ABC is circumscribed about a circle O. If R, S, and T are the three points at which the triangle is tangent to the circle, then what is the value of x + y?

(A) 180

(B) 210

(C) 240

(D) 270 ✓

(E) It cannot be determined from the information given.

If $\overline{AC}$ is tangent to O at R, ∠ARO = 90°

If $\overline{AB}$ is tangent to O at S, ∠ASO = 90°

∠ROS = 90°

360° – 90° = 270°

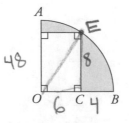

48

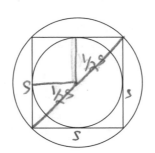

37. In the figure above, *AB* is an arc of a circle with center *O*. If the length of arc *AB* is 5π and the length of *CB* is 4, what is the sum of the areas of the shaded regions?

(A) 25π – 60
(B) 25π – 48 ✓
(C) 25π – 36
(D) 100π – 48
(E) 100π – 36

$5\pi \qquad C = 20\pi$

$\frac{1}{4}\pi r^2 = 5\pi \qquad 20\pi = 2\pi r$

$\frac{1}{4}r^2 = 5 \qquad 10 = r$

$\frac{1}{4}100\pi = 25\pi$

$25\pi - 48$

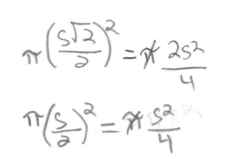

38. In the figure above, the smaller circle is inscribed in the square and the square is inscribed in the larger circle. If the length of each side of the square is *s*, what is the ratio of the area of the larger circle to the area of the smaller circle?

(A) $2\sqrt{2} : 1$
(B) $2 : 1$ ✓
(C) $\sqrt{2} : 1$
(D) $2s : 1$
(E) $s\sqrt{2} : 1$

$\frac{s\sqrt{2}}{2} = d_L$

$s = d_s$

$\pi\left(\frac{s\sqrt{2}}{2}\right)^2 = \pi\frac{2s^2}{4}$

$\pi\left(\frac{s}{2}\right)^2 = \pi\frac{s^2}{4}$

GEOMETRY PRACTICE SET ANSWER KEY

1.	A	20.	B
2.	D	21.	D
3.	C	22.	E
4.	D	23.	D
5.	C	24.	A
6.	C	25.	A
7.	C	26.	C
8.	E	27.	B
9.	E	28.	B
10.	B	29.	D
11.	C	30.	D
12.	D	31.	D
13.	C	32.	D
14.	D	33.	B
15.	D	34.	D
16.	C	35.	E
17.	E	36.	D
18.	B	37.	B
19.	A	38.	B

EXPLANATIONS

1. The figure isn't too helpful as is, but if we extend the following lines

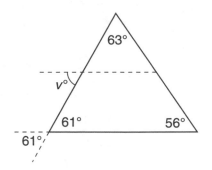

    we can form a transversal. The $v°$ angle corresponds to the 61° angle, so $v = 61$.

2. Of the eight angles created by a transversal, four are acute, four are obtuse, and every acute angle is supplementary to every obtuse angle. We are given that n, q, and s are acute (accounting for three of the four) and l and m are supplementary, so exactly one of l or m is acute and the remaining four angles are obtuse. Check Statement II first, since it appears in the most answer choices:

    II. n is acute and o is obtuse, so this statement is true. Eliminate (A) and (C).

    I. o and p are two of the unmentioned obtuse angles, so this statement is true as well. That eliminates (B) and (E), making (D) correct. For the curious:

    III. q is acute, but there is no way to tell whether l or m is obtuse, so this statement doesn't have to be true.

3. There's a lot going on in this problem, so begin with the most concrete piece of information—the area of $\triangle ABC$ is 50. $\overline{AB}$ is 10, so $\overline{BC}$ must also be 10 and $\overline{BD} = 10 + 14 = 24$. That makes $\triangle ABD$ a 5-12-13 right triangle, so $\overline{AD} = 26$.

4. If the circle were tangent to the vertical line, $\overline{AD}$ would have the same length as its radius. Since the circle is five feet from the vertical line, the radius of this circle is $15 - 5 = 10$, and its diameter is $10 \times 2 = 20$. That makes ACD a 3-4-5 right triangle, so $z = 25$.

5. The given radius isn't much help, but remember that *any* line segment from the center of a circle to its edge is a radius. To make this problem more manageable, add the following radius to the figure:

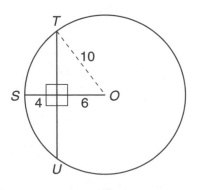

You now have a 3-4-5 right triangle, making the height of the right triangle 8. A radius that is perpendicular to a chord will bisect that chord, so $\overline{UT} = 8 \times 2 = 16$.

6. With the given information, *ABCD* can be either a rhombus or a square. A square has two qualities that a rhombus lacks—congruent diagonals and four right angles. Choice (C), if true, gives us the former, so it is correct.

7. A regular hexagon has six equal sides and six equal angles. The formula $(n - 2)180$ tells you that a hexagon has $(6 - 2)180 = (4)180 = 720°$, so each angle measures $\dfrac{720}{6} = 120°$. To find $\overline{XT}$, begin by splitting the hexagon into six triangles:

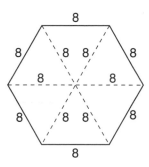

Since each angle was originally 120°, and the dotted lines bisect each of the six angles, each newly formed triangle is an equilateral triangle with sides of 8 as shown below:

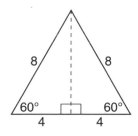

The height of each triangle is a leg of a 30-60-90 triangle with a side of 4 and a hypotenuse of 8, so the height is $4\sqrt{3}$ and $\overline{XT} = 2 \times 4\sqrt{3} = 8\sqrt{3}$.

8. Rectangle *JKLM* has two sides of 13 and a perimeter of 74, so its remaining two sides must each be $\dfrac{74 - 2(13)}{2} = \dfrac{74 - 26}{2} = \dfrac{48}{2} = 24$. So *JKLM* is a 13 × 24 rectangle, which makes the semicircle's diameter 24 and its radius 12. The area of the rectangle is 13 × 24 = 312. The area of the semicircle is $\dfrac{1}{2}\pi r^2 = \dfrac{1}{2}\pi(12)^2 = \dfrac{1}{2}(144)\pi = 72\pi \approx 226$. Therefore, the area of the entire figure is approximately 312 + 226 = 538.

9. Since each of the smaller squares has a side length of 5, and the portion of each square that doesn't overlap the circle has a length of 3, the circle's radius is 5 − 3 = 2. The area of the circle is $2^2\pi = 4\pi$, and the area of each smaller square is 5 × 5 = 25. Only $\dfrac{1}{4}$ of the circle overlaps the shaded square, so the area of the shaded region is twice the difference between the area of one smaller square minus $\dfrac{1}{4}$ the circle's area: $2\left(25 - \dfrac{4\pi}{4}\right) = 50 - 2\pi$.

10. From a geometric point of view alone, this problem seems nearly impossible. However, if you add your knowledge of proportions to the mix, it becomes much more manageable. While the large right triangle isn't much help, the two smaller ones (the ones above the squares with sides 8 and a, respectively) are much more useful. Using the provided values, we can figure out the height of each of those triangles:

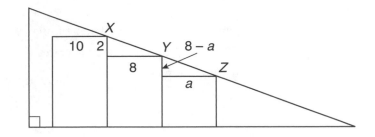

Both triangles are right triangles, and their hypotenuses lie on the same line, so the two triangles are similar. This allows us to set up the following proportion to find a:

$$\frac{2}{8} = \frac{8-a}{a}$$

$$2a = 64 - 8a$$

$$10a = 64$$

$$a = 6.4$$

11. $\triangle GEH$ is isosceles, so altitude $\overline{ED}$ must bisect the triangle. The square has a side of 3, so $\overline{GD} = \overline{DH} = 1.5$. Since $y = 2.5$, each shaded triangle is a 3-4-5 right triangle and $\overline{ED} = 2$. The area of the square is $3^2 = 9$, and the area of the shaded region is $\frac{1}{2} \times 3 \times 2 = 3$, so the area of the unshaded region is $9 - 3 = 6$.

12. The area of circle G is 25π, so G must have a radius of $\sqrt{25} = 5$, and diameter $\overline{FT}$ must have a length of $5 \times 2 = 10$. While you *could* back-solve each choice using the distance formula, it's a lot quicker to first check for a choice that matches one axis and is ten units away on the other. Choice (D) has the same x-axis as $(4, 5)$, and its y-axis of -5 is exactly ten units away, so it must be correct.

13. To find the area of the unshaded region, you'll need to subtract the area of the shaded region from the area of the entire region. Unfortunately, the entire region is not a standard figure, which makes finding its area difficult. However, if you add the following two lines to the figure, the entire region becomes a large square with its upper-right vertex at point $(9, 9)$. The area of this large square is $9 \times 9 = 81$ square units.

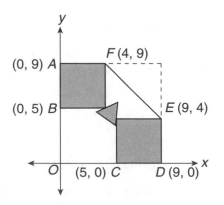

The shaded squares in the figure each have a side of 4 (the distance from $(0, 5)$ to $(0, 9)$ and the distance from $(5, 0)$ to $(9, 0)$), so the area of each square is $4 \times 4 = 16$. You were given that the shaded triangle has an area of 5, so the area of the shaded region is $16 + 16 + 5 = 37$. The area of the large square minus the area of the shaded region is $81 - 37 = 44$. This is not the answer, however, as we still need to subtract the area of the dotted isosceles right triangle in the upper right. The triangle has legs of 5 (the distance from $(4, 9)$ and $(9, 4)$ to $(9, 9)$), so its area is $\frac{1}{2} \times 5 \times 5 = 12.5$. Therefore, the area of the unshaded region is $44 - 12.5 = 31.5$.

14. To find the area of ΔFGH, you will need its base and height. The triangle is inscribed in a cube with a side length of 5, so height $\overline{FG} = 5$. The base of ΔFGH, $\overline{GH}$, happens to be the hypotenuse of ΔGHI, a right triangle with legs of 5, so ΔGHI is an isosceles right triangle and $\overline{GH} = 5\sqrt{2}$. ΔFGH has a height of 5 and a base of $5\sqrt{2}$, so its area is $\frac{1}{2} \times 5 \times 5\sqrt{2} = \frac{25\sqrt{2}}{2}$.

15. The volume of a cylinder is $\pi r^2 h$. The gravy can has a volume of $\pi(4^2)(12) = 16(12)\pi = 192\pi$. The can is only $\frac{1}{6}$ full, so the volume of the gravy is $\frac{192\pi}{6} = 32\pi$. The new can has a volume of $(2^2)(12) = 4(12)\pi = 48\pi$, so with 32π of gravy, it would be $\frac{32\pi}{48\pi} = \frac{2}{3}$ full.

16. We have three pairs of vertical angles around the point of intersection: a and d, b and e, and c and f. Therefore, $a = d$, $b = e$, and $c = f$. Let's look at the three statements one at a time.

    I. $a + b = d + e$. Since $a = d$ and $b = e$, this is true. Eliminate choice (D).

    II. $b + e = c + f$. We know that $b = e$ and $c = f$, but now how the pairs relate to each other. Statement II does not have to be true. Eliminate choices (B) and (E).

    III. $a + c + e = b + d + f$. This is true, since $a = d$, $c = f$, and $b = e$. That is, we can match each angle on one side of the equation with a different angle on the other side. Statement III must be true.

    Statements I and III must be true.

17. Since AE is a line segment, all the lengths are additive, so $AE = AD + DE$. We're told that $AD = 6$ and $AE = 8$. So $DE = AE - AD = 8 - 6 = 2$. We're also told that $BE = 6$. So $BD = BE - DE = 6 - 2 = 4$. We have the length of BD, but still need the length of BC. Since $CD = 3(BC)$, the situation looks like this:

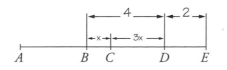

Here x stands for the length of BC. Since $BD = 4$, we can write:

$$x + 3x = 4$$
$$4x = 4$$
$$x = 1$$

18.

Before we look at the choices, let's see what information we can get from the diagram. We can see that angles p and x together are supplementary to the right angle, so p and x together must form a right angle. The same is true for the angles q and y. We also have these two pairs of vertical angles: $p = y$ and $x = q$. Now let's look at the three statements.

I. $p = x$ and $q = y$. This will be true only if $p = 45$. Since we have no way of knowing the exact measure of p, this can be true, but doesn't have to be. Eliminate choices (A), (D), and (E).

II. $x + y = 90$. This is true since $q + y = 90$ and $x = q$. Eliminate choice (C).

Since we've eliminated four answer choices, we can safely pick choice (2) without checking statement III. For practice, though, let's have a look anyway:

III. $x = y = 45$. There is no indication from the diagram that the angles x and y must have the same degree measure. Statement III does not have to be true.

Statement II only must be true.

19. The angle marked $(2x - 20)°$ and the angle marked $3x°$ together form a straight angle. This means that the sum of their degree measures must be 180.

$$(2x - 20) + (3x) = 180$$
$$2x - 20 + 3x = 180$$
$$5x = 200$$
$$x = \frac{200}{5} = 40$$

20. If $\angle DBA$ has a measure of 60°, $\angle CBD$, which is supplementary to it, must have a measure of $180 - 60$, or 120°. $\angle DCB$ has a measure of 30°; that leaves $180 - (120 + 30)$, or 30 degrees for the remaining interior angle: BDC.

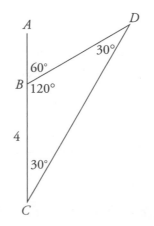

Since $\angle BCD$ has the same measure as $\angle BDC$, ΔBCD is an isosceles triangle, and the sides opposite the equal angles will have equal lengths. Therefore, BD must have the same length as BC, 4.

21.

(Note that we've added point D for clarity).

The area of a triangle is $\frac{1}{2} \times$ base $\times$ height. If we treat AB as the base of ΔABC, then the triangle's height is CD. Each square has side 1, so we can just count the squares. $AB = 1$, $CD = 4$, so the area is $\frac{1}{2} \times 1 \times 4 = 2$.

22. We know one of the sides we're given is the hypotenuse; since the hypotenuse is the longest side, it follows that it must be the larger value we're given. The side of length $\frac{d}{3}$ must be the hypotenuse, since d is positive (all lengths are positive), and $\frac{1}{3}$ of a positive value is always greater than $\frac{1}{4}$ of a positive value. Now we can use the Pythagorean theorem to solve for the unknown side, which we'll call x.

$$(\text{hypotenuse})^2 = (\text{leg})^2 + (\text{leg})^2$$

$$\left(\frac{d}{3}\right)^2 = \left(\frac{d}{4}\right)^2 + x^2$$

$$\frac{d^2}{9} = \frac{d^2}{16} + x^2$$

$$\frac{d^2}{9} - \frac{d^2}{16} = x^2$$

$$\frac{16d^2 - 9d^2}{144} = x^2$$

$$\frac{7d^2}{144} = x^2$$

$$x = \frac{d\sqrt{7}}{12}$$

Another way we can solve this, that avoids the tricky, complicated algebra is by picking a number for d. Let's pick a number divisible by both 3 and 4 to get rid of the fractions: 12 seems like a logical choice. Then the two sides have length $\frac{12}{3}$, or 4, and $\frac{12}{4}$, or 3. If one of these is the hypotenuse, that must be 4, and 3 must be a leg. Now use the Pythagorean Theorem to find the other leg:

$$(\text{leg})^2 + (\text{leg})^2 = (\text{hyp})^2$$
$$(\text{leg})^2 + (3)^2 = (4)^2$$
$$(\text{leg})^2 + 9 = 16$$
$$(\text{leg})^2 = 7$$
$$\text{leg} = \sqrt{7}$$

Now plug in 12 for d into each answer choice; the one which equals $\sqrt{7}$ is correct.

$$\frac{5 \times 12}{12} = 5 \quad \text{Discard.}$$

$$\frac{12}{\sqrt{7}} \neq \sqrt{7} \quad \text{Discard.}$$

$$\frac{12}{5} \neq \sqrt{7} \quad \text{Discard.}$$

$$\frac{12}{12} = 1 \quad \text{Discard.}$$

$$\frac{12\sqrt{7}}{12} = \sqrt{7} \quad \text{Correct.}$$

23. Drawing a diagram makes visualizing the situation much easier. Picture a ladder leaning against a building:

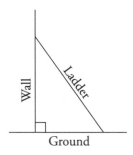

This forms a right triangle, since the side of the building is perpendicular to the ground. The length of the ladder, then, is the hypotenuse of the triangle; the distance from the foot of the building to the base of the ladder is one leg; the distance from the foot of the building to where the top of the ladder touches the wall is the other leg. We can write these dimensions into our diagram:

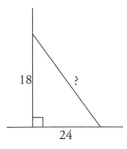

The one dimension we're missing (what we're asked to find) is the length of the ladder, or the hypotenuse. Well, we could use the Pythagorean Theorem to find that, but these numbers are fairly large, and calculating will be troublesome. When you see numbers this large in a right triangle, you should be a little suspicious; perhaps the sides are a multiple of a more familiar Pythagorean Triplet. One leg is 18 and another leg is 24; 18 is just 6 × 3, and 24 is just 6 × 4. So we have a multiple of the familiar 3-4-5 right triangle. That means that our hypotenuse, the length of the ladder, is 6 × 5, or 30.

24. This problem involves as much algebra as geometry. The Pythagorean theorem states that the sum of the squares of the legs is equal to the square of the hypotenuse, or, in this case:

$$x^2 + (x + 2)^2 = (2x - 2)^2$$

and from here on in it's a matter of algebra:

$$x^2 + x^2 + 4x + 4 = 4x^2 - 8x + 4$$
$$12x = 2x^2$$
$$2x^2 - 12x = 0$$
$$2x(x - 6) = 0$$

When the product of two factors is 0, one of them must equal 0. So we find that

EITHER	**OR**
$2x = 0$	$x - 6 = 0$
$x = 0$	$x = 6$

According to the **equation**, the value of x could be either 0 or 6, but according to the **diagram**, x is the length of one side of a triangle, which must be a positive number. This means that x must equal 6 (which makes this a 6:8:10 triangle).

Another way to do this problem is to try plugging each answer choice into the expression for x, and see which one gives side lengths which work in the Pythagorean Theorem. Choice (A) gives us 6, 8, and 10 (a Pythagorean Triplet) for the three sides of the triangle, so it must be the answer.

25.

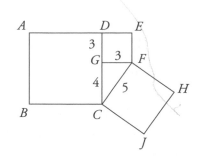

In order to determine the area of square *FCJH*, we can find the length of side *FC*, which is the hypotenuse of $\triangle FGC$. We can find the length of *FC* by finding the lengths of *FG* and *GC*.

Since *ABCD* has area 49, each side must have length $\sqrt{49}$, or 7. Therefore, *DC* has length 7. Since *DEFG* has area 9, side *FG* must have length $\sqrt{9}$, or 3. *DG* is also a side of the same square, so its length is also 3. The length of *CG* is the difference between the length of *DC* and the length of *DG*: 7 − 3 = 4. Now we have the lengths of the legs of $\triangle FGC$: 3 and 4, so this must be a 3-4-5 right triangle. So *CF* has length 5. The area of square *FCJH* is the square of the length of *CF*: $5^2 = 25$.

26. The bases of $\triangle AEB$ and $\triangle ACD$ both have the same length, since *AB* = *CD*. So we just need to find the relationship between their respective heights. *AC* and *BD* intersect at the center of the rectangle, which is point *E*. Therefore, the perpendicular distance from *E* to side *AB* is half the distance from side *CD* to side *AB*. This means that the height of $\triangle AEB$ is half the height of $\triangle ACD$. So the area of $\triangle ACD$ is twice the area of $\triangle AEB$: 2 × 8 = 16.

27. The sum of all four sides of 6*w*. The two short sides add up to $\frac{w}{2} + \frac{w}{2}$, or *w*. This leaves 6*w* − *w*, or 5*w*, for the **sum** of the other two sides. So **each** long side is $\frac{1}{2}(5w)$, or $\frac{5}{2}w$. So,

$$\text{Area} = \left(\frac{w}{2}\right)\left(\frac{5w}{2}\right) = \frac{5w^2}{4}$$

28. The best way to solve this problem is to pick a value for the length of a side of square *A*. We want our numbers to be easy to work with, so let's pick 10 for the length of each side of square *A*. The length of each side of square *B* is 100 percent greater, or twice as great as a side of square *A*. So the length of a side of square *B* is 2 × 10, or 20. The length of each side of square *C* is 50 percent greater, or $1\frac{1}{2}$ times as great as a side of square *B*.

So the length of a side of square *C* is $1\frac{1}{2}$ × 20, or 30. The area of square *A* is 10^2, or 100. The area of square *B* is 20^2, or 400. The sum of the areas of squares *A* and *B* is 100 + 400, or 500. The area of square *C* is 30^2, or 900. The area of square *C* is greater than the sum of the areas of squares *A* and *B* by 900 − 500, or 400. The percent that the area of square *C* is greater than the sum of the areas of squares *A* and *B* is $\frac{400}{500}$ × 100%, or 80%.

29. First of all, if a rectangle has perimeter 10, what could its dimensions be? Perimeter = 2L + 2W, or 2(L + W). The perimeter is 10, so 2(L + W) = 10, or L + W = 5. Since L and W must be integers, there are two possibilities: L = 4 and W = 1 (4 + 1 = 5), or L = 3 and W = 2 (3 + 2 = 5). Let's consider each case separately. If L = 4, then how many of these rectangles would fit along the length of the larger rectangle? The length of the larger rectangle is 60: 60 ÷ 4 = 15, so 15 smaller rectangles would fit, if they were lined up with their longer sides against the longer side of the large rectangle. The width of the smaller rectangles is 1, and the width of the large rectangle is 24, 24 ÷ 1 = 24, so 24 small rectangles can fit against the width of the large rectangle. The total number of small rectangles that fit inside the large rectangle is the number along the length times the number along the width: 15 × 24 = 360. In the second case, L = 3 and W = 2. 60 ÷ 3 = 20, so 20 small rectangles fit along the length; 24 ÷ 2 = 12, so 12 small rectangles fit along the width. So the total number of small rectangles is 20 × 12, or 240. We're asked for the greatest number, which we got from the first case: 360.

30. The fastest method is to pick a value for the diameter of the circle. Let's suppose that the diameter is 4. Then the radius is $\frac{4}{2}$, or 2, which means that the area is $\pi(2)^2$, or 4π. Increasing the diameter by 50% means adding on half of its original length: 4 + (50% of 4) = 4 + 2 = 6. So the new radius is $\frac{6}{2}$, or 3, which means that the area of the circle is now $\pi(3)^2$, or 9π. The percent increase is $\frac{9\pi - 4\pi}{4\pi} \times 100\% = \frac{5\pi}{4\pi} \times 100\%$, or 125%.

31. Since the lighthouse can be seen in all directions, its region of visibility is a circle with the lighthouse at the center. Before the change, the light could be seen for 60 miles, so the area of visibility was a circle with radius 60 miles. Now it can be seen for 40 miles further, or for a total of 60 + 40, or 100 miles. The area is now a circle with radius 100 miles:

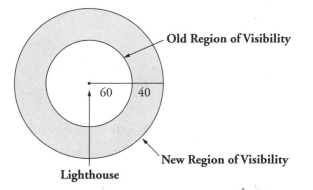

The increase is just the difference in these areas; that is, the shaded region on the above diagram.

$$\text{Increase} = \text{New area} - \text{old area}$$
$$= \pi(100)^2 - \pi(60)^2$$
$$= 10{,}000\,\pi - 3{,}600\,\pi$$
$$= 6{,}400\,\pi$$

The value of π is a bit more than 3, so 6,400 π is a bit more than 3 × 6,400, or just over 19,200. The only choice close to this is 20,000.

32. Let's call the end-points of the arc *A* and *B* and the center of the circle *C*. Major arc *AB* represents $\frac{3}{4}$ of 360°, or 270°. Therefore, minor arc *AB* is 360° − 270°, or 90°. Since *AC* and *CB* are both radii of the circle, △*ABC* must be an isosceles right triangle:

We can find the distance between *A* and *B* if we know the radius of the circle. Major arc *AB*, which takes up $\frac{3}{4}$ of the circumference, has a length of 12π, so the entire circumference is 16π. The circumference of any circle is 2π times the radius, so a circle with circumference 16π must have radius 8. The ratio of a leg to the hypotenuse in an isosceles right triangle is 1:$\sqrt{2}$. The length of *AB* is $\sqrt{2}$ times the length of a leg, or 8$\sqrt{2}$.

33. We're looking for the length of *CD*. Note that *OC* is a radius of the circle, and if we knew the length of *OC* and *OD*, we could find *CD*, since *CD* = *OC* − *OD*. Well, we're given that *OB* has a length of 10, which means the circle has a radius of 10, and therefore *OC* is 10. All that remains is to find *OD* and subtract. The only other piece of information we have to work with is that *AB* has length 16. How can we use this to find *OD*? If we connect *O* and *A*, then we create two right triangles, △*ADO* and △*BDO*:

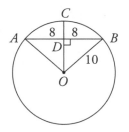

Since both of these right triangles have a radius as the hypotenuse, and both have a leg in common (*OD*), then they must be equal in size. Therefore, the other legs, *AD* and *DB*, must also be equal. That means that *D* is the midpoint of *AB*, and so *DB* is $\frac{1}{2}$(16), or 8.

Considering right triangle *BDO*, we have a hypotenuse of 10 and a leg of 8; thus the other leg has length 6. (It's a 6-8-10 Pythagorean Triplet.) So *OD* has length 6, and *CD* = 10 − 6 = 4.

34. Connect the centers of the circles *O*, *P*, and *Q* as shown. Each leg in this right triangle consists of two radii. The hypotenuse consists of two radii plus the diameter of the small circle.

We can find the radii of the large circles from the given information. Since the total area of the four large circles is 36π, each large circle has area 9π. Since the area of a circle is πr^2, we know that the radii of the large circles all have length 3.

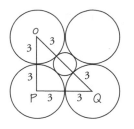

Therefore, each leg in the isosceles right triangle *OPQ* is 6. The hypotenuse then has length $6\sqrt{2}$. (The hypotenuse of an isosceles right triangle is always $\sqrt{2}$ times a leg.) The hypotenuse is equal to two radii plus the diameter of the small circle, so $6\sqrt{2} = 2(3) +$ diameter, or diameter $= 6\sqrt{2} - 6$.

35.

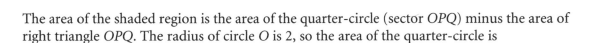

The area of the shaded region is the area of the quarter-circle (sector *OPQ*) minus the area of right triangle *OPQ*. The radius of circle *O* is 2, so the area of the quarter-circle is

$$\frac{1}{4}\pi r^2 = \frac{1}{4} \times \pi(2)^2 = \frac{1}{4} \times 4\pi = \pi$$

Each leg of the triangle is a radius of circle *O*, so the area of the triangle is

$$\frac{1}{2}bh = \frac{1}{2} \times 2 \times 2 = 2$$

Therefore, the area of the shaded region is $\pi - 2$.

36.

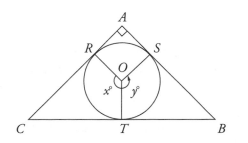

A line tangent to a circle is perpendicular to the radius of the circle at the point of tangency. Since *AC* is tangent to circle *O* at *R* and *AB* is tangent to circle *O* at *S*, $\angle ARO$ and $\angle ASO$ are 90° angles. Since three of the angles in quadrilateral *RASO* are right angles, the fourth, $\angle ROS$, must also be a right angle. $\angle ROS$, x, and y sum to 360°, so we can set up an equation to solve for $x + y$.

$$x + y + 90 = 360$$
$$x + y = 360 - 90$$
$$x + y = 270$$

37. The total area of the shaded regions equals the area of the quarter-circle minus the area of the rectangle. Since the length of arc AB (a quarter of the circumference of circle O) is 5π, the whole circumference equals $4 \times 5\pi$, or 20π. Thus, the radius OE has length 10. (We've added point E in the diagram for clarity.) Since OB also equals 10, $OC = 10 - 4$, or 6. This tells us that $\triangle OEC$ is a 6-8-10 right triangle and $EC = 8$.

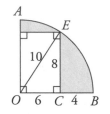

Now we know the dimensions of the rectangle, so we can find its area: area $= l \times w = 8 \times 6 = 48$. Finally, we can get the total area of the shaded regions:

$$\text{Area of shaded regions} = \frac{1}{4} \times \pi \times (10)^2 - 48$$
$$= 25\pi - 48$$

38. The length of each side of the square is given as s. A side of the square has the same length as the diameter of the

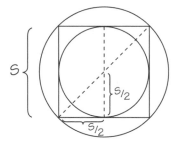

smaller circle. (You can see this more clearly if you draw the vertical diameter in the smaller circle. The diameter you draw will connect the upper and lower tangent points where the smaller circle and square intersect.) This means that the radius of the smaller circle is $\frac{s}{2}$, so its area is $\left(\frac{s}{2}\right)^2 \pi$, or $\frac{s^2}{4}\pi$. Now draw a diagonal of the square, and you'll see that it's the diameter of the larger circle. The diagonal breaks the square up into two isosceles right triangles, where each leg has length s as in the diagram above. So the diagonal must have length $s\sqrt{2}$.

Therefore, the radius of the larger circle is $\frac{s\sqrt{2}}{2}$, so its area is $\left(\frac{s\sqrt{2}}{2}\right)^2 \pi$, or $\frac{2s^2}{4}\pi$, or $\frac{s^2}{2}\pi$. This is twice the area of the smaller circle.

section two

THE QUANTITATIVE SECTION

CHAPTER FOUR

Quantitative Comparisons

Angst...bedlam...consternation...disquiet. These words and more describe the mind-set of the average GRE test taker when faced with the eccentric nature of Quantitative Comparisons. (Incidentally, those are great vocabulary words to know for the Verbal section!) For most folks, change is bad, and QCs represent the biggest change from the format of the ACT or SAT math that they are so used to. To make matters worse, QCs are the most numerous in a section whose time restrictions feel too tight to begin with.

As an advanced test taker, you have many psychological advantages over your less-experienced peers. You thrive on change. You can remain calm enough to remember that 2 is greater than 1. You know that (E) is a horrible guess for this question type. (We know, we know, but you'd be surprised!)

So QCs should be a walk in the park for test takers of your caliber, right? Well, not necessarily. You see, QCs are the one question type where you could fall for a trap and not even realize it. Think about it: Consider the length of either a word problem or a Data Interpretation question and compare that to a QC. With the former, the length makes you feel a bit better subconsciously about digging in and spending a decent amount of time on each question. The incredible brevity of QCs, however, tends to make you feel like you aren't going fast enough. To maximize the effect, the test makers will play dirty in the hardest QCs. Make no mistake: QCs aren't about math. They are about the devious tricks and traps that are just waiting to snare the unsuspecting test taker. The focus on these questions will not be the advanced math you don't need to know—it'll be on the little quirks and pitfalls that even advanced test takers like yourself may fall for.

GRE test makers craft their finest QCs with deception, illusion, and misdirection. To claim your perfect 800 in the Quantitative section, you must learn to evade the chicanery...and we will assist you with six of our best strategies. Know them well and you'll effortlessly avoid these petty tricks on Test Day.

INSTRUCTIONS

Before we show you how to tear apart some of the nastiest Quantitative Comparisons in the history of the GRE, it's worthwhile to first take a moment to examine how they work. A typical QC consists of two columns, A and B, and may contain common information—that is, information true of both columns—centered above them. Each column features a quantity, and your job is to determine which of the following is always true:

- The quantity in Column A is greater.
- The quantity in Column B is greater.
- The two quantities are equal.
- The relationship cannot be determined from the information given.

Since the choices never change, it is definitely to your benefit to memorize them for your GRE. Doing so will save you a lot of valuable time when the clock is ticking on Test Day, and we will do our part by not printing them for the practice problems in this chapter.

Two QC Principles to Remember...

(D) is *never* correct when both columns contain only numbers.

Numbers are constant, but (D) requires a column quantity relationship that can vary.

(D) is *always* correct when the column quantity relationship can change.

(D) is correct if one of the columns is larger, smaller, or the same only *some* of the time.

KAPLAN'S 6-STEP METHOD FOR QUANTITATIVE COMPARISONS

1. Compare, don't calculate.

Especially effective when you can estimate.

2. Compare piece by piece.

Great for QCs that involve sums or products.

3. Make one column look like the other.

When columns cannot be directly compared, this is the key.

4. Do the same thing to both columns.

Adding, subtracting, multiplying, or dividing both columns by the same quantity can often make their differences easier to compare.

5. Pick numbers.

It works wonders in word problems, and it'll do the same here.

6. Redraw the diagram.

Redrawing any given diagrams can clear up the relationships between measurements.

QUANTITATIVE COMPARISONS PRACTICE SET

<u>Column A</u> <u>Column B</u>

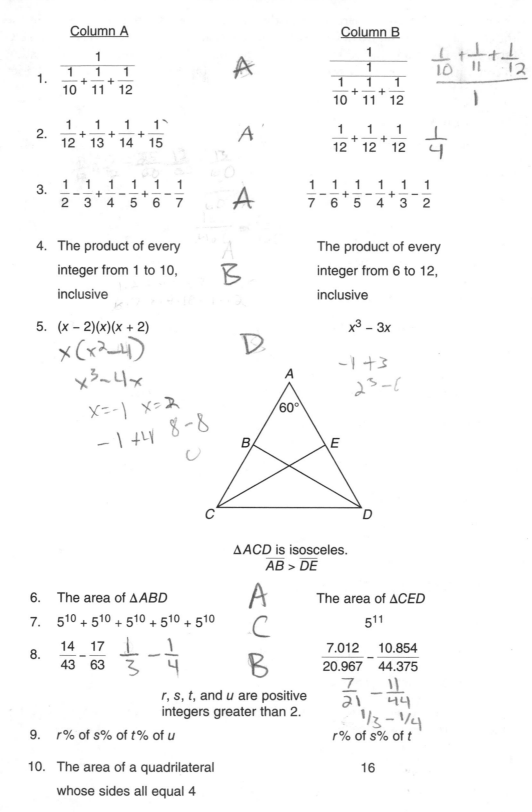

1. $\dfrac{1}{\dfrac{1}{10}+\dfrac{1}{11}+\dfrac{1}{12}}$ $\dfrac{1}{\dfrac{1}{\dfrac{1}{10}+\dfrac{1}{11}+\dfrac{1}{12}}}$

2. $\dfrac{1}{12}+\dfrac{1}{13}+\dfrac{1}{14}+\dfrac{1}{15}$ $\dfrac{1}{12}+\dfrac{1}{12}+\dfrac{1}{12}$

3. $\dfrac{1}{2}-\dfrac{1}{3}+\dfrac{1}{4}-\dfrac{1}{5}+\dfrac{1}{6}-\dfrac{1}{7}$ $\dfrac{1}{7}-\dfrac{1}{6}+\dfrac{1}{5}-\dfrac{1}{4}+\dfrac{1}{3}-\dfrac{1}{2}$

4. The product of every integer from 1 to 10, inclusive The product of every integer from 6 to 12, inclusive

5. $(x-2)(x)(x+2)$ x^3-3x

$\triangle ACD$ is isosceles.
$\overline{AB} > \overline{DE}$

6. The area of $\triangle ABD$ The area of $\triangle CED$

7. $5^{10}+5^{10}+5^{10}+5^{10}+5^{10}$ 5^{11}

8. $\dfrac{14}{43}-\dfrac{17}{63}$ $\dfrac{7.012}{20.967}-\dfrac{10.854}{44.375}$

r, s, t, and u are positive integers greater than 2.

9. $r\%$ of $s\%$ of $t\%$ of u $r\%$ of $s\%$ of t

10. The area of a quadrilateral whose sides all equal 4 16

Column A	Column B

The product of four distinct integers is 24.

11. The average of the four integers $\qquad$ 2

12. $(973 + 973)^2$ $\qquad$ $973^2 + 973^2 + 973^2 + 973^2$

13. $\sqrt{17} + \sqrt{18} + \sqrt{19}$ $\qquad$ $\sqrt{142}$

$$x^2 > y^2 > 0$$

14. $\dfrac{x}{y} - \dfrac{y}{x}$ $\qquad$ $\dfrac{y}{x} - \dfrac{x}{y}$

15. $(0.12)^{11}$ $\qquad$ $(0.11)^{12}$

16. $(41)^2 - (42 - 21)^2$ $\qquad$ $(41 - 21)^2$

$$\text{For } x \neq y, \ x \ \Phi \ y = \frac{(x + y)}{(x - y)}$$

17. $p \ \Phi \ q$ $\qquad$ $q \ \Phi \ p$

$$x^5 = -32$$

18. x^3 $\qquad$ $2x^2$

$$6 \, (10)^n > 60{,}006$$

19. n $\qquad$ 6

The product of two integers is 10.

20. The average of two integers $\qquad$ 3

The average bowling score of n bowlers is 160. The average of these n scores together with a score of 170 is 161.

21. n $\qquad$ 10

After five adults leave a party, there are three times as many children as adults. After a further 25 children leave the party, there are twice as many adults as children.

22. The original number of adults $\qquad$ 14

Remember:

(A) The quantity in Column A is greater

(B) The Quantity in Column B is greater

(C) The two quantities are equal

(D) The relationship cannot be determined from the information given

QUANTITATIVE COMPARISONS PRACTICE SET ANSWER KEY

1.	A	12.	C
2.	A	13.	A
3.	A	14.	D
4.	B	15.	A
5.	D	16.	A
6.	A	17.	D
7.	C	18.	B
8.	B	19.	D
9.	D	20.	D
10.	D	21.	B
11.	D	22.	A

EXPLANATIONS

1. As an advanced test taker, you probably *could* figure out the value of each column in a few minutes, but that's not the point. (Those of you who enjoy that kind of torture may want to see if ETS is hiring.) The key difference between QCs and other problems in the Quantitative section is that the former requires you to figure out only if one side is always bigger, smaller, or the same. Its actual value is irrelevant.

   To compare these two quantities, all you need to know is that the sum of the three fractions in the denominators of both columns is less than 1. Column A is "1 divided by less than 1," so the result will be greater than 1. Column B, the reciprocal of Column A, is essentially "1 divided by greater than 1," so its value will be less than 1. That means Column A is larger.

2. While there's no quick way to evaluate Column A, there's no need to. Recognizing that Column B is $\frac{1}{4}$, which can be rewritten as $\frac{1}{16} + \frac{1}{16} + \frac{1}{16} + \frac{1}{16}$, allows you to compare piece by piece. Each fraction in Column A is larger than $\frac{1}{16}$, so (A) is correct.

3. An ugly problem and one where you can't simply compare piece by piece. However, you may have noticed that Column B looks *very* similar to Column A, and that is the secret to busting this one in record time. Reordering the fractions in Column B gives you $-\frac{1}{2} + \frac{1}{3} - \frac{1}{4} + \frac{1}{5} - \frac{1}{6} + \frac{1}{7}$. Now factor out a -1, and Column B becomes (-1) $\left(\frac{1}{2} - \frac{1}{3} + \frac{1}{4} - \frac{1}{5} + \frac{1}{6} - \frac{1}{7}\right)$. Column A is larger.

4. If you managed to evaluate those two columns in under a minute, you have our respect (and our condolences). If not, rest assured that graduate schools are *not* looking for human calculators. The key to this problem is recognizing that both columns have $6 \times 7 \times 8 \times 9 \times 10$ in common. Dividing both columns by that leaves Column A with $1 \times 2 \times 3 \times 4 \times 5$ and Column B with 11×12. $3 \times 4 = 12$, so divide these out as well. Column A is left with $1 \times 2 \times 5 = 10$, and Column B is left with 11. (B) is correct.

5. If you divide both columns by x, you'll have $(x - 2)(x + 2) = x^2 - 4$ in Column A and $x^2 - 3$ in Column B, making (B) correct, right? Well, unfortunately, if you *did* do all that, you would've fallen right into the test maker's trap: without knowing whether x is positive or negative (it might even be 0!), you cannot simply divide it out. In this type of QC, it's best to play it safe by picking numbers. If $x = 0$, both columns would be equal. However, if $x = \pm 2$, Column A would be 0 while Column B would not, so (D) is correct.

6. An isosceles triangle with a 60° angle is equilateral, but that realization alone won't answer the question. The centered information tells you that $\overline{AB} > \overline{DE}$, so redraw the diagram exaggerating that relationship:

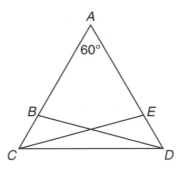

In this redrawn diagram, Column A is clearly greater, so (A) is correct.

Now see if you can find the best approach to each of the following while avoiding the traps.

7. Insanely large numbers are one of the GRE's ways of telling you not to calculate. In this problem, factoring out 5^{10} from Column A gives you $5^{10}(1 + 1 + 1 + 1 + 1) = 5^{10}(5) = 5^{11}$. The two columns are equal.

8. With such ugly fractions, remember to compare rather than calculate. While it's difficult to compare these expressions to each other, you *can* compare them both to the expression $\frac{1}{3} - \frac{1}{4}$. A bit of estimation reveals that Column A features a fraction that is slightly smaller than $\frac{1}{3}$ subtracting one that is slightly larger than $\frac{1}{4}$, while Column B has a fraction that is slightly larger than $\frac{1}{3}$ subtracting one that is slightly smaller than $\frac{1}{4}$, so Column B is larger.

9. You may have been tempted to pick (B) without thinking, as tacking another "percent of" onto the string would usually make the result smaller. (The "positive integers greater than 2" was meant to mislead you into thinking just that!) Unfortunately, the GRE doesn't reward test takers who answer without thinking, so be sure not to do that on Test Day! If u is greater than 100, Column A would be larger; if it is 100, the two would be equal; and if u is less than 100, Column B would be larger. (D) is correct.

10. "A quadrilateral whose sides all equal 4" sounds like a square, so the two columns are equal, right? Not so fast: there's one *other* type of quadrilateral with that property—a rhombus. The area of a rhombus is base × height. While this rhombus would have a base of 4, its height would be less than 4:

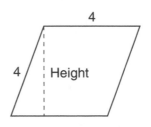

If the quadrilateral in question is indeed a rhombus, Column B would be larger. Therefore, (D) is correct.

11. If four distinct integers have a product of 24, they could be 1, 2, 3, and 4, making the average 2.5. That would make Column A larger. However, some or all of these integers could also be negative. If, for example, the integers were −1, 2, 3, and −4, their average would now be 0. (D) is correct.

12. The numbers are extremely ugly, but the solution can still be quick: Rewriting Column A as $(2 \times 973)^2$ and factoring out the 2 gives you $2^2(973^2) = 4(973^2)$. Column B can be rewritten as $4(973^2)$ as well, so the two columns are equal.

13. Column A is difficult to evaluate quickly, but Column B is a little less than $\sqrt{144} = 12$. $12 = 4 + 4 + 4$, and each of the terms in Column A is greater than 4, so Column A is larger.

14. Lots of variable expressions are present here, so pick numbers to be safe. If $x = 3$ and $y = 2$, Column A would be $\frac{3}{2} - \frac{2}{3}$ (a positive value) and Column B would be $\frac{2}{3} - \frac{3}{2}$ (a negative value), so Column A would be larger. If $x = -3$ and $y = 2$, Column A would be $\frac{-3}{2} - \frac{2}{-3} = -\frac{3}{2} + \frac{2}{3}$ (a negative value) and Column B would be $\frac{2}{-3} - \frac{-3}{2} = -\frac{2}{3} + \frac{3}{2}$ (a positive value), so Column B would be larger. With no way to tell, (D) is correct.

15. With positive values less than 1, the higher the power you raise it to, the smaller it gets. Column A has a larger base and a smaller exponent, so it must be larger.

16. You should have decided immediately there must be a shortcut here; multiplying out the values of the columns would take too long. (It may also have occurred to you that the answer cannot be (D)—since all you are dealing with here are numbers, there must be some way to compare the columns, even if you do have to calculate the values.) So you might have asked yourself whether the columns look like anything familiar. In fact, Column A looks a lot like a difference of squares. It can be factored, then, into

    $(41)^2 - (21)^2 = (41 - 21)(41 + 21) = (20)(62)$

    Now, how does this compare to $(41 - 21)^2$ or $(20)^2$ in Column B? Column A is larger: 20×62 is larger than 20×20.

17. Picking numbers will help you solve this problem. With symbolism problems like this, it sometimes helps to put the definition of the symbol into words. For this symbol, you can say something like "$x \Phi y$ means take the sum of the two numbers, and divide that by the difference of the two numbers." One good way to do this problem is to pick some values. You know that p is positive and q is negative. So suppose p is 1 and q is −1. Figure out what $p \Phi q$ is first. You start by taking the sum of the numbers, or $1 + (-1) = 0$. That's the numerator of the fraction, and you don't really need to go any further than that. Whatever their difference is, since the numerator is 0, the whole fraction must equal 0. (The difference can't be 0 also, since $p \neq q$.) So that's $p \Phi q$; now what about $q \Phi p$? Well, that's going to have the same numerator as $p \Phi q$: 0.

    The only thing that changes when you reverse the order of the numbers is the denominator of the fraction. So $q \Phi p$ has a numerator of 0, and that fraction must equal 0 as well. So you've found a case where the columns are equal. Try another set of values, and see whether the columns are always equal. If $p = 1$ and $q = -2$, then the sum of the numbers is $1 + (-2)$ or -1. So that's the numerator of the fraction in each column. Now for the denominator of $p \, \Phi \, q$ you need $p - q$ or $1 - (-2) = 1 + 2 = 3$. Then the value of $p \, \Phi \, q$ is $-\frac{1}{3}$. The denominator of $q \, \Phi \, p$ is $q - p$ or $-2 - 1 = -3$. In that case, the value of $q \, \Phi \, p$ is $-\frac{1}{3}$ or $\frac{1}{3}$. In this case, the columns are different; therefore, the answer is (D).

18. Start by working with the sign of x, and hope that you won't have to go any further than that. If x^5 is negative, then what is the sign of x? It must be negative—if x were positive, then any power of x would also be positive. Since x is negative, Column A, x^3, which is a negative number raised to an odd exponent, must also be negative. But what about Column B? Whatever x is, x^2 must be positive (or zero, but we know that x can't be zero); therefore, the quantity in Column B must be positive. We have a positive number in Column B and a negative number is Column A; Column B must be greater.

19. Divide both sides of the inequality by 6. We're left with $(10)n > 10,001$, which can also be written at $104 + 1$, so we know that $(10)n > 104 + 1$. Therefore, the quantity in Column A, n, must be 5 or greater. Column B is 6; since n could be less than, equal to, or greater than 6, we need more information.

20. The best place to start here is with pairs of integers that have a product of 10. The numbers 5 and 2 have a product of 10, as do 10 and 1, and the average of each of these pairs is greater than 3, so you may have thought that (A) was the correct answer. If so, you should have stopped yourself, saying, "That seems a little too easy for such a late QC question. They're usually trickier than that." In fact, this one was. There's nothing in the problem that limits the integers to positive numbers: they can just as easily be negative. The numbers -10 and -1 also have a product of 10, but their average is a negative number—in other words, less than Column B. We need more information here; the answer is (D).

21. A quick way to analyze a problem such as this one is to realize that the additional bowler with a score of 170 is raising everyone else's average by one point from 160 to 161. Her score is $161 + 9$, so she has 9 extra points that she can distribute to the remaining bowlers by which to raise their scores. Therefore, she can raise the average score of exactly 9 other bowlers from 160 to 161, so $n = 9$ and Column B is greater.

22. Start by setting the columns equal. Suppose there were originally 14 adults at the party. Then after 5 of them leave, there are $14 - 5$ or 9 adults left. There are 3 times as many children as adults, so there are 3×9 or 27 children. Then 25 children leave the party, so there are $27 - 25$ or 2 children left. So 9 adults and 2 children remain at this party. Is that twice as many adults as children? No, it is more than 4 times as many. So this clearly indicates that the columns can't be equal—but does it mean that Column A is bigger or Column B is bigger? Probably the simplest way to decide is to pick another number for the original number of adults, and see whether the ratio gets better or worse. Suppose we start with 13 adults. After 5 adults leave, there are $13 - 5$ or 8 adults. Multiplying 3 times 8 gives 24 children. Now if 25 children leave, we're left with $24 - 25$ or -1 children. But that's no good; how can you have a negative number of children? This means we've gone the wrong way; our ratio has gotten worse instead of better. So 14 isn't right for the number of adults, and 13 is even worse, so the correct number must be something more than 14, and Column A is bigger.

CHAPTER FIVE

Word Problems

Ahh…word problems—the GRE Math question type that mere test-taking mortals fear. To them, word problems are hopelessly complex contraptions designed to effortlessly entangle them before the math even begins. Their verbiage, sporting English alongside math, is often enough to make novice test takers surrender without a fight.

As an advanced test taker, you are not so easily frightened by these word problems. You are able to pierce through the illusion of difficulty by translating English into math. You have nothing to fear. Or do you? For there exist word problems that seem no less difficult even when their armor of English has been hacked away. Ones that give even the best test takers pause. We will show them to you…and you will face them here.

But fear not, advanced test taker. We will provide you with Kaplan's proven method and three tools—three devastating Kaplan strategies—to aid you in this daunting task. Master these and it will be the word problems that have reason to fear you.

Word Problem Strategies

Here's the general approach to any word problem:

1. **Read through the whole question.** Do this to get a sense of what's going on. You want to know the basic situation described, the type of information you've been given, and—most important of all—what exactly you are being asked.

2. **Identify the different variables or unknowns and label them.** For example, if the problem discusses Charlie's and Veronica's warts, you may wish to use "c" to represent Charlie's warts and "v" to represent Veronica's warts. Notice that we didn't use "x" and "y." If we had, we might later forget whether x represented Charlie's warts or Veronica's.

3. **Translate the problem into math.** This usually entails rewriting the English sentences into equations or statements. The sentence "Veronica has four fewer warts than Charlie has" would become: $v = c - 4$. Notice that the math terms are not in the same order as the English terms in the sentence. When you translate, you are translating the ideas. The idea here is "four fewer warts than Charlie." That means $c - 4$, not $4 - c$!

4. **Tackle the math.** Solve the equations. Determine the value that the question is asking you for.

5. **Check your work, if you have time.**

The Translation Table

It's a good idea to familiarize yourself with the mathematical meanings of some of the most common words used in word problems. Knowing these equivalencies can provide you with a specific, concrete starting point, especially when a word problem seems incomprehensible.

The table below can be a lifesaver—the sort of thing you might want to tattoo on your inside forearm. But that would be wrong.

English	"Mathish"
equals is, was, will be has costs adds up to is the same as	=
times of multiplied by product of twice, double, triple, half	×
per out of divided by each ratio of __ to __	÷
and plus added to sum combined total	+
minus subtracted from less than decreased by difference between	−
what how much how many a number	x, n, (variable)

Remember: If you are completely baffled by a word problem, look for some of the words in the left-hand column. Then work from their math equivalent and try to construct an equation.

KAPLAN'S 3-STEP METHOD FOR WORD PROBLEMS

Step 1: Read through the question carefully.
Nothing is more frustrating (and embarrassing) than doing the right work and answering the wrong question!

Step 2: Choose your approach.
Sometimes it'll be easier to just "do the math." Other times it won't.

Step 3: Ensure that you answered the right question before confirming your answer.
Once you confirm, you can't go back, so check first!

PICKING NUMBERS

For abstract word problems—ones that use variables, either expressed or implied, rather than numbers—picking numbers is often the ideal strategy. While a little bit of algebra never hurt anyone (especially advanced test takers like yourself!), slogging through the variables and abstractions while the clock is running is the quickest way to make the kinds of careless mistakes that will keep you from that coveted 800 on the Quantitative section. So why take that risk?

The most difficult part of an abstract word problem tends to be the abstraction itself. Picking numbers takes care of that by replacing the abstraction with concrete numbers of your choosing. Picking numbers in difficult abstract problems is not only faster, it is also a lot less error-prone, and *that* is especially important when shooting for a perfect score. Here's how it works:

Step 1: Pick numbers that are permissible and manageable to stand in for the variables.

Step 2: Answer the question using the number(s) you picked.

Step 3: Plug your numbers into each choice, eliminating those that give a different result.

Step 4: Repeat steps 1–3 with a different set of numbers if more than one choice remains.

So what does it mean for numbers to be *permissible* and *manageable*?

Permissible refers to numbers that abide by the restrictions in the problem (e.g., if you're told that $x > y$, don't pick a larger value for y than for x).

Manageable refers to numbers that are small and easy to work with. While you *could* pick numbers like 264,598, 362,094, and 926,037 over numbers like 1, 2, and 3, it defeats the original purpose of making the problem easier. (You masochists out there can rest assured that the math will still work out.)

Question 1

1. For her final exam, Martha needed to memorize the formula $g = \dfrac{a^3 b}{c^2}$. During the exam, however, she accidentally halved the value of b and doubled the value of c. Martha's final value for g is what fraction of the correct value?

   (A) $\dfrac{1}{64}$

   (B) $\dfrac{1}{32}$

   (C) $\dfrac{3}{64}$

   (D) $\dfrac{1}{16}$

   (E) $\dfrac{1}{8}$

Question 2

2. To prepare for his class presentation, Roman needs to find a mathematical phenomenon to talk about. After hours of thought, he decides on a number. What fascinates Roman about this number is that dividing it by 2 leaves a remainder of 1, dividing it by 3 leaves a remainder of 2, and dividing it by 4 leaves a remainder of 3. What is the remainder when dividing the number by 5?

   (A) 0

   (B) 1

   (C) 2

   (D) 3

   (E) 4

Questions 1 and 2: Answers and Explanations

Explanation: Martha's Final

1. Poor Martha. With so many variables to keep track of, it's no wonder she mixed them up on

Test Day. Let's give her a hand by picking 1 for a, 2 for b, and 3 for c. Now the correct value for g

would be $\dfrac{1^3 \times 2}{3^2} = \dfrac{1 \times 2}{9} = \dfrac{2}{9}$. After accidentally halving b and doubling c, Martha's value for g would

be $\dfrac{1^3 \times 1}{6^2} = \dfrac{1}{36}$. Therefore, Martha's value for g is $\dfrac{1}{36} \div \dfrac{2}{9} = \dfrac{1}{36} \times \dfrac{9}{2} = \dfrac{1}{8}$ of the correct value.

Explanation: Roman's Numeral

2. Roman may have spent hours searching for his number, but you won't have that luxury on the GRE. The best way to approach this problem is to pick a number with the same characteristics as Roman's. Let's start with the last characteristic—a remainder of 3 when divided by 4.

The smallest number that satisfies that characteristic is 4 + 3 = 7. While 7 shares the first characteristic—as would any odd number—it leaves a remainder of 1 only when divided by 3. So 7 doesn't work.

The next smallest number we can try is (4 × 2) + 3 = 8 + 3 = 11. This is also an odd number, so the first characteristic is fine, and 11 ÷ 3 does leave a remainder of 2. So 11 meets all the requirements for Roman's numeral. Dividing 11 by 5 leaves a remainder of 1, so (B) is correct.

Picking numbers is useful when...

...there are variables (expressed or implied) in both the question and the choices.
...the question tests a number property you do not recall.
...the question and the choices both involve either fractions or percents.

BACK-SOLVING

Sometimes abstraction in a problem is really not the problem. Sometimes the question in the word problem is simple and clear, but the equation you need to answer it is difficult to set up and/or work with. Sometimes there's simply no easy way to pick numbers. For these times, Kaplan recommends back-solving.

The main difference between GRE word problems and ones that might show up on an ordinary math test is that the former will always provide you with five answer choices. No matter how difficult the problem before you seems, the realization that the correct answer *must* be one of the five choices on the page allows you to back-solve—that is, to work backward from the answer choices to the problem. Here's how you do that:

Step 1: Estimate whether the answer will be small or large.

Step 2: Start with (B) or (D).

Step 3: If necessary, test the choice that you did not start with.

Why should you start with (B) or (D), as opposed to (C), which is right in the middle of the pack? By starting with (B) or (D), your chances of getting the correct answer in a single try double. Here's why: if you start with (C), there are three possibilities: (C) is right, (C) is too small, or (C) is too big. Only the first scenario produces a correct answer; the other two require more testing.

But by starting with (B) or (D), you increase your chances of getting the right answer on the first try by taking advantage of the format of GRE answers: they're listed in order of ascending size.

For example, if you start with (B), you have these three possibilities: (B) is right, (A) is right (because (B) is too big), or (B) is too small. If you start with (D), the possibilities are: (D) is right, (E) is right (because (D) is too small), or (D) is too big.

Either way, you have a 40 percent likelihood of locating the correct answer on your first try, compared to a 20 percent likelihood of success when you start with (C). If you apply the "Do I think the answer will be small or big?" question first, you can greatly improve your chances of hitting the correct answer in one shot.

If (B) is too small or (D) is too large (in other words, you guessed wrong on the "small or big" estimate), you'll have three choices left. In either case, testing the middle remaining choice immediately reveals the correct answer. For example, if you started with (B) and it was too small, you'd be left with (C), (D), or (E). If (D) turns out to be too small, (E) is correct. If it's too large, (C) is correct. By following this system, you won't have to test more than two of the five choices. In fact, you'll usually have to test only one.

3. Each week at a local supermarket, Manager *A* is paid a flat $25 per hour while Manager *B* is paid $20 per hour for the first 30 hours and 50% more for each additional hour. If both managers worked the same number of hours and received the same pay on a certain week, how many hours did each manager work that week?

(A) 36

(B) 42

(C) 54

(D) 60

(E) 68

4. Each time Stacy visits MCA Theaters, she gets either the small popcorn or the large popcorn. The ratio of the number of times Stacy chooses the small popcorn over the large is 5 to 2. The price of the small popcorn is $5, and the price of the large popcorn is $11. If Stacy spent a total of $235 on popcorn at the theater this year, how many times did she choose the large popcorn?

(A) 7

(B) 10

(C) 16

(D) 19

(E) 24

Questions 3 and 4: Answers and Explanations

Explanation: Equivalent Pay

3. Manager *B* gets the short end of the stick for a grueling 30 hours before things start looking up, so the two most likely worked for a large number of hours. So start by back-solving from choice (D):

Manager *A* gets $25 × 60 = $1,500 for 60 hours of work.

Manager *B* gets $20 × 30 = $600 for the first 30 hours of work and ($20 × 1.5) × (60 − 30) = $30 × 30 = $900 for the remaining 30 hours. That's a total paycheck of $600 + $900 = $1,500.

That's equal pay for equal work, so the two must have worked 60 hours each, and we found that in one try! Had you started with (B), you would've found it to be too small (Manager *A*, with her flat rate, would still be making more), and your next step would've been to test (D).

Explanation: Popcorn Sizes

4. With a complex problem in the question stem and simple numbers in the answer choices, this is a great problem to backsolve. Two hundred thirty-five dollars may be a lot of money, but with popcorn prices like that, Stacy probably didn't get too much for her money, so let's start with (B):

If Stacy chose the large 10 times, it would have cost her $10 \times \$11 = \$110$. The 5-to-2 ratio would mean choosing the small popcorn 25 times, which costs $25 \times \$5 = \$125$, for a total popcorn bill of $\$110 + \$125 = \$235$. That's what she spent, so (B) is correct.

If you had started with (D), you would've found the total bill to be much larger than $235, which would prompt you to test (B) next.

Backsolving is useful when . . .

> . . . the main difficulty in the problem is actually setting it up.
> . . . the actual question is fairly simple and the choices are all numbers.
> . . . there is no easy way to know which numbers you can pick.

ELIMINATION

How quickly can you solve this problem?

5. Alicia can paint 7 houses in 16 hours while Kate can do the same in 12 hours. Working at those rates, how many hours would it take the two of them to paint 14 houses together?

(A) $13\dfrac{5}{7}$

(B) 17

(C) $19\dfrac{4}{7}$

(D) 21

(E) $22\dfrac{2}{7}$

As an advanced test taker, you're probably familiar with the combined work formula, which would allow you to solve this problem in about a minute. But what if it's the very last problem in the section and you don't *have* a minute? What if you can't remember how to "work" the combined work formula under such pressure? What if you didn't even know of such a thing?

With no real way to pick numbers or backsolve here, such a problem could be your nemesis—the one that keeps you from that perfect 800. However, if you stay calm and apply the final strategy, you could blow past this problem in record time *without needing any advanced math.*

Explanation: Question 5

Explanation: Paint the House

5. If Alicia can paint 7 houses in 16 hours, *two* Alicias would be able to paint 14 houses in the same 16 hours. Instead of having a clone of herself as a helper, Alicia has Kate, who is *faster* than another Alicia. Hence, Alicia + Kate should be able to paint 14 houses in *fewer* hours than the 16 it takes Alicia + Alicia. Only (A) is less than 16, so it *must* be correct, and you didn't need any math to get it!

For the math way, you'll need the combined work formula: $\dfrac{A \times B}{A+B}$, where A and B are the times it takes each person to complete her task. For 7 houses, Alicia needs 16 hours and Kate needs 12, so $A = 16$ and $B = 12$. The amount of time it takes the two to finish 7 houses together is:

$$\frac{16 \times 12}{16 + 12} = \frac{192}{28} = \frac{48}{7} = 6\frac{6}{7} \text{ hours}$$

To finish 14 houses, they would need twice that, or $\dfrac{48}{7} \times 2 = \dfrac{96}{7} = 13\dfrac{5}{7}$ hours. As you can see, the math way takes a while and is much more prone to error.

How about the following percents problem?

6. Four friends—Alan, Jen, Larry, and Tina—each have a certain amount of money. Alan has 25% of Jen's total, Jen has 50% of Larry's total, and Larry has 80% of Tina's total. What percent of Tina's total does Alan have?

   (A) 10%
   (B) 15%
   (C) 20%
   (D) 25%
   (E) 35%

Explanation: Question 6

Explanation: Dollars and Percents

6. The unknown amounts in this percents problem may have prompted you to pick numbers, but elimination is *much* faster: Tina has the most cash, while poor Alan (no pun intended) has only 25% of Jen's total, so he clearly has less than 25% of Tina's total. That leaves three-way action with (A), (B), and (C), right? Not quite: Jen has only half of what Larry (who has less than Tina) has, so Alan's percent of Tina must be less than half of his percent of Jen. Half of 25% is 12.5%, and only (A) is less than that, so it must be correct!

To see the math, pick numbers. If Tina starts with $100, Larry (with 80% of her total) has $100 × .8 = $80, Jen (with 50% of Larry's total) has $80 × .5 = $40, and Alan (with 25% of Jen's total) has $40 × .25 = $10. $10 is 10% of Tina's $100.

Now you may ask, "If elimination is that quick and powerful, why bother having the other strategies at all?" The answer is that elimination works on fewer problems than either picking numbers or backsolving. When it works, it is the quickest method by far. When it doesn't, the other two methods and even the straightforward math are good to fall back on. Elimination isn't for every question, but the huge savings in time, along with the satisfaction you'll get from sneaking by the question without resorting to math, are priceless.

Elimination Is Useful When...

> ...the choices are spaced far apart.
> ...there is no easy way to pick numbers or back-solve.
> ...you recognize the number property tested.

Now that we're walked you through the first six word problems, let's see if you can find the most efficient approach to each of the following practice problems.

Word Problems Practice Set

7. On Tuesday, Ralf's skydiving class is scheduled to have their first test jump. In the figure below, the square with an inscribed circle represents the landing zone into which Ralf will be jumping. If Ralf lands on a random spot in this zone and landing in the shaded regions means failure, what is the probability that Ralf will not fail?

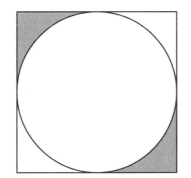

(A) $\dfrac{2-\pi}{16}$

(B) $\dfrac{2+\pi}{16}$

(C) $\dfrac{4-\pi}{8}$

(D) $\dfrac{4+\pi}{8}$

(E) $\dfrac{8+\pi}{4}$

8. Adam, Beth, Carol, and David are throwing a bag of marbles to each other while running toward a tree. When Adam throws the bag to Beth, $\frac{1}{3}$ of the original number of marbles fall out of the bag before Beth catches it. When Beth throws the bag to Carol, $\frac{1}{4}$ of the original number of marbles fall out of the bag before Carol catches it. When Carol throws the bag to David, $\frac{1}{5}$ of the original number of marbles fall out of the bag before David catches it. When David reaches the tree, he looks inside the bag and finds fewer than 20 marbles. How many marbles were originally in the bag?

   (A) 30
   (B) 44
   (C) 60
   (D) 72
   (E) 140

9. At a recent regional meeting, the director of Oranj Orange discussed the possibility of diluting the company's orange juice further to increase profits. Oranj Orange currently produces orange juice that's 80% juice by volume. If the director proposes combining q quarts of their current juice with o quarts of real orange juice and w quarts of water, which of the following represents the percent of juice by volume of this new mixture?

   (A) $80(q + o + w)\%$

   (B) $\dfrac{80}{q+o}\%$

   (C) $\dfrac{80q}{o+w}\%$

   (D) $\dfrac{80o}{q+o+w}\%$

   (E) $\dfrac{80q+100o}{q+o+w}\%$

10. During a recent thunderstorm, a bolt of lightning damages an old fudge machine at Freddie's Fudge Factory. The machine produces 40 fudge popsicles per hour with a maintenance cost of $4 per hour, and it would cost $8,000 to repair it. Instead of fixing the damaged machine, Freddie could also opt to purchase a new state-of-the-art model for $20,000. If the new machine has an output capacity of 60 fudge popsicles per hour and a maintenance cost of $3 per hour, how many fudge popsicles would Freddie need to make before buying the new machine becomes more profitable than fixing the old one? (Assume that the cost of materials for the fudge popsicles is negligible.)

   (A) 40,000
   (B) 75,000
   (C) 120,000
   (D) 195,000
   (E) 240,000

11. Rachel has *d* dollars under her mattress. She took out $24 yesterday, added $56 two days ago, took out $63 three days ago, and added $12 four days ago. How many dollars did Rachel have under her mattress before adding the $12 four days ago?

    (A) $d - 155$

    (B) $d - 87$

    (C) $d - 19$

    (D) $d + 19$

    (E) $d + 155$

12. On the first Monday of the year, each of Wana Village's *r* residents would contribute equally to raise a community fund of *c* dollars. Unfortunately, a flash flood wiped out a large amount of livestock this year, making it impossible for *l* residents to contribute. If the community fund is to remain the same, which of the following represents the additional amount that each remaining resident must contribute?

    (A) $\dfrac{c - l}{r}$

    (B) $\dfrac{c}{r - l}$

    (C) $\dfrac{r\,l}{c - r}$

    (D) $\dfrac{c\,l}{r(r - l)}$

    (E) $\dfrac{cr}{r(r - l)}$

13. At Crusty's Burgers, a burger, fries, and a small soda cost $6.00 while a burger, fries, and an ice-cream float cost $9.00. If the small soda and the fries cost the same and the ice-cream float costs three times as much as either one, how much is the burger?

    (A) $1.00

    (B) $1.50

    (C) $2.50

    (D) $3.00

    (E) $4.00

14. At 9:00 A.M., the Springfeld Roadster leaves *ABC* Station for *XYZ* Depot traveling at a constant speed of 120 mph. At 10:30 A.M., the Tootin' Tycoon leaves *XYZ* Depot for *ABC* Station traveling at a constant speed of 200 mph. If both trains increase their speeds by 25% when they meet at noon, when will the Springfeld Roadster reach its destination?

    (A) 1:00 P.M.

    (B) 1:30 P.M.

    (C) 2:00 P.M.

    (D) 2:30 P.M.

    (E) 3:00 P.M.

15. Last Saturday, Angela and Margaret had to mow their neighbor's lawn. Working together, the two of them finished the job in 6 hours. If it would have taken Angela 10 hours to mow the lawn by herself, how many hours would it have taken Margaret?

    (A) 8
    (B) 12
    (C) 15
    (D) 24
    (E) 32

16. The total fare for 2 adults and 3 children on an excursion boat is $14.00. If each child's fare is one half of each adult's fare, what is the adult fare?

    (A) $2.00
    (B) $3.00
    (C) $3.50
    (D) $4.00
    (E) $4.50

17. Doris spent $\frac{2}{3}$ of her savings on a used car, and she spent $\frac{1}{4}$ of her remaining savings on a new carpet. If the carpet cost her $250, how much were Doris' original savings?

    (A) $1,000
    (B) $1,200
    (C) $1,500
    (D) $2,000
    (E) $3,000

18. Gheri is n years old. Carl is 6 years younger than Gheri and 2 years older than Jean. What is the sum of the ages of all three?

    (A) $3n + 16$
    (B) $3n + 4$
    (C) $3n - 4$
    (D) $3n - 8$
    (E) $3n - 14$

19. A class of 40 students is to be divided into smaller groups. If each group is to contain 3, 4, or 5 people, what is the largest number of groups possible?

    (A) 8
    (B) 10
    (C) 12
    (D) 13
    (E) 14

KAPLAN

20. Philip has twice as many salamanders as Matt. If Philip gives Matt 10 of his salamanders, he will have half as many as Matt. How many salamanders do Philip and Matt have together?

    (A) 10
    (B) 20
    (C) 30
    (D) 40
    (E) 60

21. In a group of 60 workers, the average salary is $80 a day per worker. If some of the workers earn $75 a day and all the rest earn $100 a day, how many workers earn $75 a day?

    (A) 12
    (B) 24
    (C) 36
    (D) 48
    (E) 54

22. Pipe *A* can fill a tank in 3 hours. If pipe *B* can fill the same tank in 2 hours, how many minutes will it take both pipes to fill $\frac{2}{3}$ of the tank?

    (A) 30
    (B) 48
    (C) 54
    (D) 60
    (E) 72

23. A factory cut its labor force by 16 percent, but then increased it by 25 percent of the new amount. What was the net percent change in the size of the workforce?

    (A) a 5% decrease
    (B) no net change
    (C) a 5% increase
    (D) a 9% increase
    (E) a 10% increase

24. If snow falls at a rate of x centimeters per minute, how many hours would it take for y centimeters to fall?

    (A) $\dfrac{x}{60y}$

    (B) $\dfrac{y}{60x}$

    (C) $\dfrac{60x}{y}$

    (D) $\dfrac{60y}{x}$

    (E) $60xy$

25. If a dealer had sold a stereo for $600, he would have made a 20 percent profit. Instead, the dealer sold it for a 40 percent loss. At what price was the stereo sold?

    (A) $300
    (B) $315
    (C) $372
    (D) $400
    (E) $440

26. If four men working at the same rate can do $\dfrac{2}{3}$ of a job in 40 minutes, how many minutes would it take one man working at this rate to do $\dfrac{2}{5}$ of the job?

    (A) 80
    (B) 88
    (C) 92
    (D) 96
    (E) 112

27. Bob and Alice can finish a job together in three hours. If Bob can do the job by himself in five hours, what percent of the job does Alice do?

    (A) 20%
    (B) 30%
    (C) 40%
    (D) 50%
    (E) 60%

WORD PROBLEMS PRACTICE SET ANSWER KEY

7.	D	18.	B
8.	C	19.	D
9.	E	20.	D
10.	E	21.	B
11.	D	22.	A
12.	D	23.	A
13.	D	24.	B
14.	C	25.	A
15.	C	26.	D
16.	A	27.	C
17.	D		

EXPLANATIONS

7. It's Ralf's big day and you get to help him succeed. Unfortunately for him (and you), the dimensions of the landing zone components aren't known. No need to panic, however, as geometric probability doesn't need exact measurements—relative ones will suffice. The easiest way to get relative measurements is to simply pick numbers for the unknowns. Let's pick 4 for the side length of the square. That would give the circle a radius of 2. The area of the square is $4 \times 4 = 16$. To find the probability of landing success, you'll need to divide the area of the unshaded region by the area of the square. To find *that*, you'll need the area of the shaded region first. (Phew! Maybe skydiving *is* easier than math!)

The area of the circle is $\pi(2)^2 = 4\pi$. Subtracting that figure leaves us $16 - 4\pi$ for the area of the square's four corner pieces. Failure is two pieces, so its area is $\frac{16-4\pi}{2} = 8 - 2\pi$. The success area is the area of the square minus the area of failure, or $16 - (8 - 2\pi) = 8 + 2\pi$. Therefore, the probability of Ralf landing in success is $\frac{8+2\pi}{16} = \frac{4+\pi}{8}$.

8. You *could* back-solve this problem, but elimination is much faster: since only whole marbles can fly out of the bag, the original number must have been a multiple of 3, 4, and 5. (B) is not a multiple of 3, (A) and (E) are not multiples of 4, and (D) is not a multiple of 5. That means (C) must be the original number of marbles in the bag.

To see the math, let's back-solve (C): Adam's toss loses $\frac{1}{3} \times 60 = 20$ marbles, Beth's toss loses $\frac{1}{4} \times 60 = 15$ marbles, and Carol's toss loses $\frac{1}{5} \times 60 = 12$ marbles. That leaves $60 - (20 + 15 + 12) = 60 - 47 = 13$ marbles, which is indeed fewer than 20.

9. Oh, that greedy director! While the plan seems to be a simple one, the math behind it is a bit more confusing with all the variables thrown around. Fortunately, the abundance of variables allows you to pick numbers. Since we're dealing with percents, let's pick 100 for q, 20 for o, and 30 for w. That gives us $.8(100) + 20 = 80 + 20 = 100$ quarts of juice in $100 + 20 + 30 = 150$ quarts of liquid, which is $\frac{100}{150} \times 100\% = \frac{2}{3} \times 100\% = \frac{200}{3}\%$ juice by volume. You can immediately eliminate (A), as multiplication and addition of whole numbers cannot lead to an improper fraction. Now plug these values into the remaining choices and look for a match:

(B) $\frac{80}{100+20}\% = \frac{80}{120}\% = \frac{2}{3}\% \neq \frac{200}{3}\%$. Eliminate.

(C) $\frac{80(100)}{20+30}\% = \frac{80(100)}{50}\% = 80(2)\% = 160\% \neq \frac{200}{3}\%$. Eliminate.

(D) $\frac{80(20)}{100+20+30}\% = \frac{1600}{150}\% = \frac{32}{3}\% \neq \frac{200}{3}\%$. Eliminate.

(E) $\frac{80(100)+100(20)}{100+20+30}\% = \frac{100(80+20)}{150}\% = \frac{2(100)}{3}\% = \frac{200}{3}\%$. This works.

Only (E) works, so it must be correct.

10. If you're going to spend money, you might as well get something new and shiny, right? That's Freddie's reasoning, and you're here to help him figure out how long (in fudge pops) it would take before the new purchase is justified. To do that, let's begin by figuring out the cost to crank out fudge pops with the two machines. The old machine cranks out 40 fudge pops per hour at a maintenance cost of $4 per hour, so each pop costs $\frac{\$4}{40} = \$0.10$. The new machine spits out 60 fudge pops per hour at a maintenance cost of $3 per hour, so each pop costs $\frac{\$3}{60} = \$0.05$. Freddie saves $0.10 – $0.05 = $0.05 per pop with the new machine. The new machine costs $20,000 – $8,000 = $12,000 more than fixing the old one (that's a LOT of nickels!), so Freddie would need to make $\frac{\$12,000}{\$0.05} = 240,000$ fudge popsicles before the purchase becomes the better decision.

11. The math itself isn't that hard, but moving backward in time makes it really easy to make a careless mistake. The problem can be solved in a number of ways, but by far the quickest way is elimination.

    The first thing you need to determine is if Rachel had *more* or *fewer* dollars under the mattress four days ago than she does now. Without even calculating, we can see that the withdrawal amounts outweigh the deposits, as $63 > $56 and $24 > $12. That means she had *more* money four days ago, so eliminate (A), (B), and (C). Now the question is whether she had $19 more or $155 more. The latter is much too large (it's actually the sum of all four amounts given), so (D) is correct.

    To see the math, start with d and work backward in time: Rachel has d dollars today, $d + 24$ yesterday (withdrew $24 to get d), $d + 24 – 56 = d – 32$ two days ago (added $56 to get $d + 24$), $d – 32 + 63 = d + 31$ three days ago (withdrew $63 to get $d – 32$), and $d + 31 – 12 = d + 19$ four days ago (added $12 to get $d + 31$).

12. The abundance of variables in both the question stem and the answer choices makes it clear that you should pick numbers. Let's pick 5 for r, 100 for c, and 3 for l. Five villagers contributing to a fund of $100 is $100 \div 5 = $20 per villager. If 3 of them can't contribute, the remaining $5 – 3 = 2$ villagers would each need to contribute $100 \div 2 = $50, which is a $50 – $20 = $30 increase per contribution. Now test out the choices:

    (A) $\dfrac{100 - 3}{5} = \dfrac{97}{5} \neq 30$. Eliminate.

    (B) $\dfrac{100}{5 - 3} = \dfrac{100}{2} = 50 \neq 30$. Eliminate.

    (C) $\dfrac{5(3)}{100 - 5} = \dfrac{15}{95} = \dfrac{3}{19} \neq 30$. Eliminate.

    (D) $\dfrac{100(3)}{5(5 - 3)} = \dfrac{20(3)}{2} = 10(3) = 30$. Keep this.

    (E) $\dfrac{100(5)}{5(5 - 3)} = \dfrac{100}{2} = 50 \neq 30$. Eliminate.

    Only (D) works, so it must be correct.

13. Simple amounts in the choices make this an excellent candidate for back-solving. With a $6.00 burger meal, a good portion of that is likely to go to the burger, so start with (D):

    If the burger is $3.00 and the fries cost the same as the soda, then the soda and fries are each $1.50. In the $9.00 meal, a $3.00 burger and $1.50 fries leave $9.00 − ($3.00 + $1.50) = $9.00 − $4.50 = $4.50 for the ice-cream float. This is indeed three times the price of the soda, so (D) is correct. Had you started with (B), the soda would've been too expensive for the ice-cream float to be three times its price.

14. When the two trains meet at noon, the Tootin' Tycoon will have traveled for 1.5 hours at 200 mph, for a total distance of 200 × 1.5 = 300 miles. This is the additional distance that the Springfeld Roadster needs to travel to reach *XYZ* Depot. With 300 miles to go, the Roadster increases its speed by 25%, so this last leg of the trip will be at 120 × 1.25 = 150 mph. At this speed, it'll take the Roadster another 300 ÷ 150 = 2 hours, so it should arrive at *XYZ* Depot at 2:00 P.M.

15. This is a difficult problem with no easy way to pick numbers or back-solve; fortunately, elimination comes to the rescue. If the two worked at the same pace, it would take each of them 6 × 2 = 12 hours to do the job on their own. Angela gets it done in only 10 hours, which is a bit faster than 12 but still fairly close to it, so Margaret must take a bit *longer* than 12. (A) and (B) are too quick, while (D) and (E) would be *way* too long, so (C) must be correct.

    For the math way, Angela needs 10 hours to mow the lawn solo, so at 6 hours, she would be $\frac{6}{10}$ done, meaning Margaret must have mowed $1-\frac{6}{10}=\frac{4}{10}$ of the lawn in those 6 hours. If it takes Margaret 6 hours to mow $\frac{4}{10}$ of the lawn, it would take her $6\times\frac{10}{4}=15$ hours to mow the whole lawn alone.

16. If each adult's fare is twice as much as each child's fare, then 2 adult fares costs as much as 4 child fares. So the 2 adult fares are as expensive as 4 children's fares. This, added to the 3 children's fares, gives us a total of 4 + 3 or 7 children's fares. This equals the $14. If 7 children's fares cost $14, then the cost of each child's fare is $\frac{14}{7}$ or $2. Adult fares cost twice as much or $4.

17. The $250 that Doris spent on the carpet is one quarter of the one-third of Doris's savings that's left over after she buys the car, or $\frac{1}{4}\times\frac{1}{3}=\frac{1}{12}$ of her original savings. Therefore, her original savings must have been 12 × $250 or $3,000.

18. Gheri is *n* years old. Carl is 6 years younger than Gheri, or *n* − 6 years old. Jean is 2 years younger than Carl, or *n* − 6 − 2 = *n* − 8 years old. The sum of their ages is then *n* + (*n* − 6) + (*n* − 8) = 3*n* − 14 years.

19. We will get the maximum number of groups by making each group as small as possible. Each group must have at least 3 people in it, so divide 40 by 3 to find the number of 3-person groups. 40 ÷ 3 = 13 with a remainder of 1. So we have 13 groups with 1 person left over. Since each group must have at least 3 people, we must throw the extra lonely student in with one of the other groups. So we have 12 groups with 3 students each, and one group with 4 students, for a maximum total of 13 groups.

20. Let p represent Philip's salamanders and m Matt's salamanders. If Philip has twice as many salamanders as Matt, we can write

$$p = 2m$$

If Philip gives Matt 10 salamanders, then he will have 10 fewer, or $p - 10$, and Matt will have 10 more or $m + 10$. In this case Philip would have half as many as Matt, so

$$p - 10 = \frac{1}{2}(m + 10)$$

We have two equations with two variables. (Note that although the number of salamanders each owns has changed, the variables p and m still have the same meaning: the original number of salamanders.) We can solve for p and m. Substitute our first expression for p, that is $p = 2m$, into the second equation and solve for m.

$$2m - 10 = \frac{1}{2}(m + 10)$$
$$4m - 20 = m + 10$$
$$3m = 30$$
$$m = 10$$

Since $p = 2m$, if $m = 10$, then $p = 20$. The total number of salamanders is $p + m = 20 + 10$ or 30.

21. If the average salary of the 60 workers is $80, the total amount received by the workers is 60 × $80 or $4,800. This equals the total income from the $75 workers plus the total income from the $100 workers. Let x represent the number of $75 workers.

Since we know there are 60 workers altogether, and everyone earns either $75 or $100, then $60 - x$ must earn $100. We can set up an equation for the total amount received by the workers by multiplying the rate times the number of workers receiving that rate and adding:

$$75x + 100(60 - x) = 4,800$$

Solve this equation to find x, the number of workers earning $75.

$$75x + 6,000 - 100x = 4,800$$
$$-25x = -1,200$$
$$25x = 1,200$$
$$x = 48$$

There were 48 workers earning $75.

22. Find how many hours it takes both pipes to fill the entire tank, multiply by $\frac{2}{3}$, then convert to minutes. If pipe A fills the tank in 3 hours, it fills $\frac{1}{3}$ of the tank in one hour. Pipe B fills

the tank in 2 hours; it must fill $\frac{1}{2}$ of the tank in one hour. So in one hour the two pipes fill $\frac{1}{2} + \frac{1}{3}$, or $\frac{5}{6}$ of the tank. If in one hour they fill $\frac{5}{6}$ of the tank, they need the inverse of $\frac{5}{6}$ or $\frac{6}{5}$ hours to fill the entire tank. It will take them $\frac{2}{3}$ of this amount of time to fill $\frac{2}{3}$ of the tank, or $\frac{2}{3} \times \frac{5}{6} = \frac{4}{5}$ of an hour.

Now convert to minutes. How many minutes is $\frac{1}{5}$ of an hour? 5 goes into 60 twelve times so $\frac{1}{5}$ of an hour is 12 minutes, and $\frac{4}{5}$ of an hour is 4 × 12 or 48 minutes. (Or one can convert directly by multiplying 60 minutes by $\frac{4}{5}$ and get $\frac{4}{5} \times 60 = 48$ minute.)

23. Choose a sample value easy to work with; see what happens with 100 jobs. If the factory cuts its labor force by 16%, it eliminates 16% of 100 jobs or 16 jobs, leaving a work force of 100 − 16 or 84 people. It then increases this work force by 25%. 25% of 84 is $\frac{1}{4}$ of 84 or 21. The factory adds 21 jobs to the 84 it had, for a total of 105 jobs. Since the factory started with 100 jobs and finished with 105, it gained 5 jobs overall. This represents $\frac{5}{100}$ or 5% of the total we started with. There was a 5% increase.

24. **Method I:**

First figure out how many minutes it would take for y centimeters of snow to fall. The snow is falling at a constant rate of x centimeters per minute; set up a proportion to find how long it takes for y centimeters. The ratio of minutes passed to centimeters fallen is a constant.

$$\frac{1 \text{ minute}}{x \text{ centimeters}} = \frac{m \text{ minute}}{y \text{ centimeters}}$$

Solve for m.

$$m \text{ minutes} = y \text{ centimeters} \bullet \frac{1 \text{ minute}}{x \text{ centimeters}}$$

$$m \text{ minutes} = \frac{y}{x} \text{ minutes}$$

Now we must convert from $\frac{y}{x}$ minutes to hours. Since hours are larger, we must divide the minutes by 60.

$$\frac{y}{x} \text{ minutes} \times \frac{1 \text{ hour}}{60 \text{ minutes}} = \frac{y}{60x}$$

Always be sure to keep track of your units: as long as they are in the right places, you can be sure you are using the correct operation.

Method II:

First find out how long it takes for *1* centimeter of snow to fall. We will eventually have to convert from minutes to hours, so we might as well do it now. If *x* centimeters of snow fall every minute, then 60 times as much will fall in an hour, or 60*x* centimeters of snow. Then one centimeter of snow will fall in the reciprocal of 60*x*, or $\frac{1}{60x}$ hours. We're almost at the end: 1 centimeter falls in $\frac{1}{60x}$ hours, so *y* centimeters will fall in *y* times as many hours, or $\frac{y}{60x}$ hours.

25. *Method I:*

Find the cost of the stereo to the dealer, then subtract 40% of this to find the price it was sold for. The selling price equals the dealer's cost plus the profit. The dealer would have made a 20% profit if he had sold the stereo for $600; therefore, letting *x* represent the cost to the dealer,

$$600 = x + 20\% \text{ of } x$$
$$600 = 120\% \text{ of } x$$
$$600 = \frac{6}{5}x$$
$$x = \frac{5}{6} \cdot 600 = 500$$

Instead the dealer sold the stereo at a loss of 40%. Since 40% or $\frac{2}{5}$ of 500 is 200, he sold the stereo for $500 − $200 = $300.

Method II:

Let *x* represent the dealer's cost. Then we're told that $600 represents *x* + 20% of *x* or 120% of *x*. We want the value of *x* − (40% of *x*) or 60% of *x*. Since 60% of *x* is one-half of 120% of *x*, the sale price must have been one-half of $600, or $300.

26. First find how long it takes 4 men to complete the entire job, then from that we can find the time for 1 man, and then we can find how long it takes 1 man to do $\frac{2}{5}$ of the job.

If 4 men can do $\frac{2}{3}$ of a job in 40 minutes, they still have $\frac{1}{3}$ of the job to do. Since they have $\frac{1}{2}$ as much work left as they have already done, it will take them $\frac{1}{2}$ as much time as they've already spent, or another 20 minutes. This makes a total of 60 minutes for the 4 men to finish the job. One man will take 4 times as long, or 240 minutes. He'll do $\frac{2}{5}$ of the job in $\frac{2}{5}$ as much time, or $\frac{2}{5} \times 240 = 96$ minutes.

Or, first determine how long it takes one man to do the job, and from this find how long it would take him to do $\frac{2}{5}$ of it. If 4 men do $\frac{2}{3}$ of the job in 40 minutes, 1 man does $\frac{1}{4}$ of this work or $\frac{1}{4} \times \frac{2}{3} = \frac{1}{6}$ of the job in 40 minutes. Therefore, it takes him 6 times as long to do the whole job, or $6 \times 40 = 240$ minutes. Again, he'll do $\frac{2}{5}$ of the job in $\frac{2}{5} \times 240 = 96$ minutes.

27. Here, work with the portion of the job Bob completes in one hour when he and Alice work together. Bob can do the job in 5 hours; he completes $\frac{1}{5}$ of the job in 1 hour. So in the 3 hours they both work, Bob does $3 \times \frac{1}{5}$, or $\frac{3}{5}$ of the job. Alice does the rest, or $1 - \frac{3}{5} = \frac{2}{5}$ of the job. The percent equivalent of $\frac{2}{5}$ is 40%. Alice does 40% of the job.

CHAPTER SIX

Oddball Word Problems

As with other GRE question types, perhaps even more so, Word Problems are often oddballs. Because they deal with "real world" situations, word problems can be used to test just about every math and logic skill under the sun. You wouldn't be properly prepared for the Advanced-level math questions if your practice didn't include a sampling of these.

On test day, of course, you may encounter other oddballs. That's just the nature of the game. But bear in mind that just because a question seems completely new to you, it doesn't have to be difficult.

Now that you've mastered advanced word problems, let's practice with some oddballs.

ODDBALL WORD PROBLEMS PRACTICE SET 1

1. A computer is programmed to generate two numbers according to the following scheme: The first number is to be a randomly selected integer from 0 to 99; the second number is to be an integer which is less than the square of the units digit of the first number. Which of the following pairs of numbers could NOT have been generated by this program?

    (A) 99, 10
    (B) 60, –10
    (C) 58, 63
    (D) 13, 11
    (E) 12, 3

2. A certain clock rings two notes at quarter past the hour, four notes at half past, and six notes at three-quarters past. On the hour, it rings eight notes plus an additional number of notes equal to whatever hour it is. How many notes will the clock ring between 1:00 P.M. and 5:00 P.M., including the rings at 1:00 and 5:00?

    (A)   87
    (B)   95
    (C) 102
    (D) 103
    (E) 115

3. Each of three charities in Novel Grove Estates has 8 persons serving on its board of directors. If exactly 4 persons serve on 3 boards each and each pair of charities has 5 persons in common on their boards of directors, then how many distinct persons serve on one or more boards of directors?

    (A)   8
    (B) 13
    (C) 16
    (D) 24
    (E) 27

ODDBALL WORD PROBLEMS PRACTICE SET 2

As if there weren't enough real math in the world, the test makers sometimes make up their own, "phony" math. Don't let it throw you. The question will always provide the information you need.

Questions 4–5 refer to the following definition.

The "connection" between any two positive integers a and b is the ratio of the smallest common multiple of a and b to the product of a and b. For instance, the smallest common multiple of 8 and 12 is 24, and the product of 8 and 12 is 96, so the connection between 8 and 12 is $\frac{24}{96} = \frac{1}{4}$.

4. What is the connection between 12 and 21 ?

    (A) $\frac{1}{9}$

    (B) $\frac{1}{7}$

    (C) $\frac{1}{3}$

    (D) $\frac{4}{7}$

    (E) $\frac{1}{1}$

5. The positive integer y is less than 20 and the connection between y and 6 is equal to $\frac{1}{1}$. How many possible values of y are there?

    (A) 7
    (B) 8
    (C) 9
    (D) 10
    (E) 11

And how about a final pair, before leaving Problem Solving for good?

ODDBALL WORD PROBLEMS PRACTICE SET 3

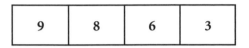

| 9 | 8 | 6 | 3 |

6. The figure above shows an example of a 4-digit identification code used by a certain bank for its customers. If the digits in the code must appear in descending numerical order, and no digit can be used more than once, what is the difference between the largest and the smallest possible codes?

    (A) 6,666
    (B) 5,555
    (C) 5,432
    (D) 4,444
    (E) 1,111

7. A machine is made up of two components, *A* and *B*. Each component either works or fails. The failure or nonfailure of one component is independent of the failure or nonfailure of the other component. The machine works if at least one of the components works. If the probability that each component works is $\frac{2}{3}$, what is the probability that the machine works?

    (A) $\frac{1}{9}$

    (B) $\frac{4}{9}$

    (C) $\frac{1}{2}$

    (D) $\frac{2}{3}$

    (E) $\frac{8}{9}$

ODDBALL WORD PROBLEMS PRACTICE SET ANSWER KEY

1. D
2. D
3. B
4. C

5. A
6. A
7. E

EXPLANATIONS

1. Don't get caught up in abstractly pondering the question stem's special instructions; turn to the answer choices and start testing the given pairs of numbers. Start at (D) or (E) for "which of the following" questions, since the GRE favors these two answer choices. (E): The units' digit of 12 is 2 and $2^2 = 4$; $4 > 3$, so eliminate. (D): The units' digit of 13 is 3, and $3^2 = 9$; $9 < 11$, so this pair does not meet the conditions, making (D) correct.

   That wasn't too bad, was it? The simple technique of backsolving allowed us to ignore all of the strangeness and focus on the task at hand.

   So there are two lessons here. One, oddball word problems can be easy word problems. And two, the basic approach to oddball word problems is to focus on what is familiar—what you know—and employ the same strategies you use for common word problem types.

   > An Advanced test taker doesn't panic when a strange word problem appears on the screen. She instead evaluates the question dispassionately, knowing that many "oddballs" are fairly easy and meant to distinguish the formulaic thinkers (who panic and screw up) from the creative thinkers (who rise to the challenge).

2. Even though the problem involves only simple arithmetic, don't try to do all the work in your head. Be systematic. Notice that the rings occur in an hourly pattern. You could set up a chart if that helps you see what's going on, or just take each part at a time by finding the number of rings at each interval of time and then adding up the total rings at each interval. The total rings on the hour $= (1 + 8) + (2 + 8) + (3 + 8) + (4 + 8) + (5 + 8) = 9 + 10 + 11 + 12 + 13 = 55$. The clock rings twice at a quarter past and it does this 4 times, so the total rings at a quarter past $= 2(4) = 8$. Likewise, the number of rings at half past $= 4(4) = 16$, and the number of rings at three-quarters past $= 6(4) = 24$. Adding up, $55 + 8 + 16 + 24 = 103$.

   You also could have set up a chart to organize information, like the one below. Setting up the chart will take a few extra seconds, but if arranging the information visually so you can see it all at once makes the difference between a confusing problem and an intuitively clear one, by all means, draw the chart, like this:

	:00	:15	:30	:45
1 P.M.	9	2	4	6
2 P.M.	10	2	4	6
3 P.M.	11	2	4	6
4 P.M.	12	2	4	6
5 P.M.	13			
Total	= 5	+ 8	+ 16	+ 24 = 103

(D) is correct.

3. To keep track of all the confusing information, set up a sketch like the one below and fill in the information as you go along.

Board 1: __ __ __ __ __ __ __ __
Board 2: __ __ __ __ __ __ __ __
Board 3: __ __ __ __ __ __ __ __

Since 4 persons serve on each board, fill in a letter for each person for 4 slots on each board; it doesn't matter where. This takes care of 4 of the 5 persons that are common to each pair of charities (1-2; 2-3; and 1-3):

Board A: A   B   C   D   __ __ __ __
Board B: A   B   C   D   __ __ __ __
Board C: A   B   C   D   __ __ __ __

Now you can fill in the fifth and sixth slots on each board with the fifth person common to each pair. And that means that the two positions left must be occupied by people who are members of only one board.

The results look like this:
Board A: A   B   C   D   E   F   H   K
Board B: A   B   C   D   E   G   I   L
Board C: A   B   C   D   F   G   J   M

Since each distinct letter represents a distinct person, just count up the number of distinct letters to get the number of distinct persons on the boards. The total number of people represented is the number of letters from A to M, and a quick count of the letters on the chart will show that this is 13. So a total of 13 persons serve on one or more boards, making (B) correct.

4. When a problem includes a special term or symbol, just follow the instructions that define it. There are two parts to a "connection": the smallest common multiple and the product. To get the smallest common multiple of 12 and 21, break each number down into its prime factors and multiply them together, counting common factors only once: $12 = 2 \times 2 \times 3$, and $21 = 3 \times 7$, giving you $2 \times 2 \times 3 \times 7$ for the least common multiple. The product of 12 and 21 is $(2 \times 2 \times 3) \times (3 \times 7)$. Therefore, the "connection" is $\dfrac{2 \times 2 \times 3 \times 7}{2 \times 2 \times 3 \times 3 \times 7}$, which reduces to $\dfrac{1}{3}$. Notice how easy it is to reduce the fraction when both the numerator and denominator are broken down into factors. (C) it is.

5. If the connection between y and 6 is $\dfrac{1}{1}$, then the smallest common multiple of y and 6 must equal the product $6y$. The lowest common multiple of two numbers equals the product of the two numbers only when there are no common factors (other than 1). Since y is a positive integer less than 20, check all the integers from 1 to 19 to see which ones have no

factors greater than 1 in common with 6: 1, 5, 7, 11, 13, 17, and 19. So there are 7 possible values for y. (A) is correct.

6. You need the difference between the largest and smallest possible codes. A digit cannot be repeated, and the digits must appear in descending numerical order. The largest such number will have the largest digit, 9, in the thousands' place, followed by the next largest digits, 8, 7, and 6, in the next three places, so 9,876 is the largest possible number. For the smallest, start with the smallest digit, 0, and put it in the ones' place. Work up from there—you end up with 3,210 as the smallest possible code. The difference between the largest and smallest codes is $9,876 - 3,210 = 6,666$, or (A).

7. The fastest way to do this is to find the probability that neither component works, and subtract that from 1. Since the probability of a component working is $\frac{2}{3}$, the probability of a component not working is $1 - \frac{2}{3} = \frac{1}{3}$. Therefore, the probability that neither component works is $\frac{1}{3} \times \frac{1}{3} = \frac{1}{9}$, and the probability that the machine works is $1 - \frac{1}{9} = \frac{8}{9}$. (E) wins.

CHAPTER SEVEN

Data Interpretation

Bars, tables, and... pies? No, we're not doing a chapter on your GRE victory party (though nothing's quite as nice as some warm apple pie after the fact!). We're talking about the section that many GRE test takers consider the most *annoying*. With a good assortment of charts and graphs, each of which contains a thousand pieces of information (okay, we might be off by a couple hundred there), a solid dose of Data Interpretation questions can be enough to drive plenty of examinees nuts. To make matters worse (as if they weren't bad enough), most of the information provided will actually be useless. In fact, if Reading Comprehension had a not-so-distant cousin in the Quantitative realm, this would be it. With "normal" Quantitative problems, the test makers will simply give you the information you need. For Data Interpretation, you'll need to dig through the junk to find it before you can even think about addressing the question.

As an advanced test taker, you are used to things not being so convenient. You eat adversity for breakfast (we like ours with cream cheese). You know how to handle a graph. Unfortunately, the test makers know that too. They know of your goal to secure that coveted 800 on the Quantitative section (we didn't tell, honest!), and they'll try to stop you with complexity and details. They'll throw everything they have at you, *including* the kitchen sink (probably on or with a table), and they'll try to mislead you.

But you'll be ready. With Kaplan's proven techniques for *efficiently* handling even the toughest that Data Interpretation has to offer, you'll be ready to claim that perfect 800 you worked so hard to achieve. Are you ready?

KAPLAN'S 4-STEP METHOD FOR DATA INTERPRETATION

Step 1: Familiarize yourself with the tables and/or graphs.

One of the most common causes of careless error in Data Interpretation is going straight to the question without first getting familiar with the data.

Step 2: Read the question stem.

With the tables and/or graphs digested, it's time to address the question.

Step 3: Locate the relevant data.

On lower difficulty problems, finding it is enough. For the tougher stuff, you'll need to manipulate the data to answer the question.

Step 4: Answer the question, approximating whenever possible.

On Data Interpretation, the GRE isn't interested in whether you can tell 31.2 from 31.23. Eyeballing charts and estimating is by far the fastest way to blow past these problems.

Four Things to Remember for Data Interpretation...

Read the title(s).

It may sound obvious, but reading the title(s) ensures that you are using the right chart.

Check the scales to see how the information is measured.

A common wrong answer type involves the right quantity in the wrong measurement.

Read any accompanying notes.

Accompanying notes, if any, are often the key to answering the questions that follow.

When a graph contains multiple lines or bars, be sure to check the legend.

Another common trap is to provide the correct quantity...for the wrong item.

TABLES

Tables are the most straightforward way to present data on the GRE. Amounts are exact, so there's no need to estimate them, but that doesn't mean that tables are necessarily easy.

Questions 1 and 2 refer to the following table.

Office Supplies Purchased per Month

	Pens (in boxes of 10)	Pencils (in boxes of 15)	Staplers
BAC Corp.	3	2	9
DFI Inc.	5	3	3
SKF Ltd.	5	2	6
ZZF LLC	4	4	1

1. Pens and pencils weigh 4 grams each, while a stapler weighs 50 grams. If shipping is $0.05 per gram, how much more would BAC Corp. pay for shipping than DFI Inc.?

   (A) $0.15
   (B) $1.00
   (C) $3.25
   (D) $5.35
   (E) $8.00

2. If an office supply unit consists of either one pen, one pencil, or one stapler, which of the following must be true?

   (A) SKF Ltd. has the fewest office supply units.
   (B) ZZF LLC has the most office supply units.
   (C) BAC Corp. has the most office supply units.
   (D) DFI Inc. has the most office supply units.
   (E) DFI Inc. has the fewest office supply units.

Questions 1 and 2: Answers and Explanations

Explanation: Shipping Costs

1. There's a lot going on here, so be sure to take things one step at a time. You could begin by summing the weight of each company's order, but it's much faster to simply keep a running tally of weight differences. Pens are 4 grams apiece, and BAC needs two fewer boxes than DFI, or $2 \times 10 \times 4 = 80$ grams less. Pencils are also 4 grams apiece, and BAC needs one fewer box than DFI, or $1 \times 15 \times 4 = 60$ grams less. Staplers weigh 50 grams each, and BAC needs six more staplers than DFI, or $6 \times 50 = 300$ grams more, for a net weight difference of $300 - 80 - 60 = 160$ grams. At $0.05 per gram, that's an additional shipping charge of $160 \times \$0.05 = \$8.00$.

Explanation: Unit Measure

2. The question is a bit vague, but the answer choices all focus on the company with either the most or the fewest office supply units, so begin by finding the company with the most and fewest units. Staplers come individually, and no company needs more than nine of them, so their number is largely irrelevant unless there's a tie. BAC is tied for fewest pencil boxes, and it has the fewest boxes of pens, so BAC must have the fewest number of office supply units. The most office supply units will be either DFI or ZZF, as both have eight boxes of pens and pencils combined, more than any other company. ZZF has more of it in pencils, so (B) is correct.

BAR GRAPHS

Bar graphs are a visual alternative to a table. While their data may not be as exact, they *do* allow you to gauge relative values with a quick glance. Bars can be either vertical or horizontal.

Questions **3 and 4** refer to the following graph.

Congressional Voter Registration by Region

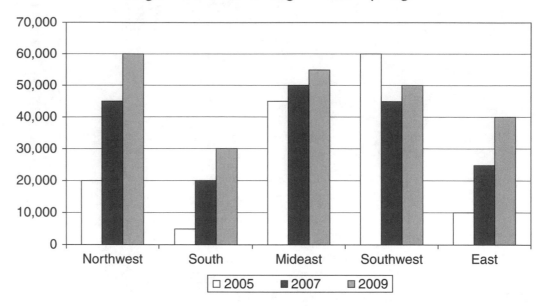

3. Which region experienced the largest percent increase in voter registration from 2005 to 2009?

   (A) Northwest
   (B) South
   (C) Mideast
   (D) Southwest
   (E) East

4. If voter turnout is traditionally 75% of voter registration, in which year did voter turnout exceed 225,000?

   (A) 2005
   (B) 2007
   (C) 2009
   (D) Voter turnout didn't exceed 225,000 in any of the three years.
   (E) Voter turnout exceeded 225,000 in all three years.

Questions 3 and 4: Answers and Explanations

Explanation: Registration Spike

3. Questions like these are excellent examples as to why you should always read the question carefully. This one is looking for the greatest *percent* increase, which is not necessarily the greatest *numerical* increase. A quick glance at the bar graph allows you to immediately eliminate (A), (C), and (D). In 2009, the Eastern region had four times as many voters as in 2005, while the Southern region had roughly six times as many for the same time period, so (B) is correct.

Explanation: Voting on the Whole

4. You *could* go about summing up the years and getting 75% of each total, but a bit of critical thinking can help you avoid all of that. With a 75% turnout, a voter turnout of 225,000 requires a voter registration of $225{,}000 \div 75\% = 225{,}000 \div \dfrac{3}{4} = 225{,}000 \times \dfrac{4}{3} = 300{,}000$. The tallest bar on the graph is 60,000, and there are five regions voting each year. The only way to reach even 300,000 registrants is for all five regions to average 60,000 registrants each. Since that is clearly not the case, (D) is correct.

LINE GRAPHS

Line graphs are another visual alternative to tables. They carry the same advantages and disadvantages as bar graphs, but their values are represented with points rather than bars.

Questions 5 and 6 refer to the following graph.

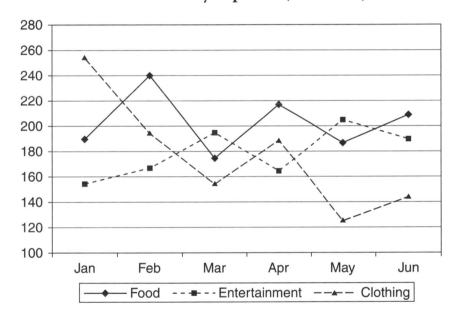

Mark's Monthly Expenses (in Dollars)

5. According to the chart, which of the following events is mostly likely to be true?

   (A) Mark got into rock music in March, causing him to spend twice as much on entertainment that month than he did in January.

   (B) Mark cut entertainment expenses in April to buy the boom box he wanted in May.

   (C) In May, Mark had to replace most of his clothes when a sudden fire destroyed them.

   (D) Mad cow disease discovered in March sparked a price increase in beef.

   (E) Mark had more free time to go to concerts and movies in February than in May.

6. If Mark's clothing expense in July is greater than his food expense in March but less than his entertainment expense in June, which of the following could be his clothing expense in July?

(A) $157

(B) $163

(C) $182

(D) $198

(E) $206

Questions 5 and 6: Answers and Explanations

Explanation: A Likely Story

5. The question seems complicated, but it's actually just a fairly simple question in disguise. The choice that's "most likely to be true" is the one that goes with the trend from the graph, so let's examine each choice in turn:

(A) You may have been tempted by this one, as March's entertainment point *looks* twice as high as January's. This is a trap, however, as the scale does not start at zero. A quick glance at the numbers on the vertical axis reveals that he did spend more, but nowhere near twice as much.

(B) If this is true, April's entertainment expenses should be lower than May's. A look at the graph confirms that this is indeed the case, so this choice is correct.

For the curious:

(C) Replacing most of his clothes in May would've resulted in his clothing expense skyrocketing. That is clearly not the case.

(D) While beef is certainly not the only food Mark can buy (he might even be a vegan), this isn't very likely, as February had the lowest food expense.

(E) More free time to go in February doesn't mean going more often, but it also doesn't make it likely for Mark to have a *lower* entertainment expense in February either.

Explanation: Clothing for the Future

6. With all the different lines and months, this question can easily confuse, so take it slow. The food expense in March is roughly halfway between the 150 and 200 marks, so Mark's March food expense is roughly $175. The July clothing expense is higher than this, so eliminate (A) and (B). The June entertainment expense is a bit under the 200 mark (around 190 or so), and Mark spent less than this on clothing in July, so (D) and (E) are way too much. That leaves (C), the correct answer.

PIE CHARTS

Pie charts differ from bar and line graphs in one very important aspect—they depict percentages rather than numbers, so be especially careful when questions compare actual amounts.

Questions **7** and **8** refer to the following pie chart.

April 2009 U.S. Fresh Fruit Imports by Weight

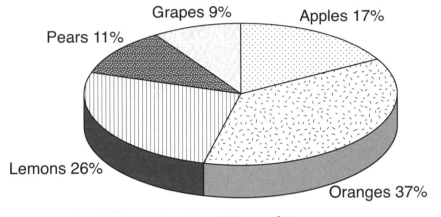

100% = 55,000 pounds

7. If apples are $2 per pound and lemons are $3 per pound, how much more was spent on lemons?

    (A) $14,300
    (B) $19,700
    (C) $24,200
    (D) $31,200
    (E) $42,900

8. If the government unveils a new plan to double its imports on grapes, oranges, and pears while eliminating its imports on apples and lemons in May, approximately what percentage of the total fresh fruit imports in May would be grapes?

    (A) 7%
    (B) 10%
    (C) 16%
    (D) 21%
    (E) 25%

Questions 7 and 8: Answers and Explanations

Explanation: Paying More for Lemons

7. The ugly numbers in this problem may have given you pause, but as with most Data Interpretation questions, the key is to estimate rather than calculate. Lemons make up 26% while apples constitute 17%, so there are 26% − 17% = 9% more lemons. 10% of 55,000 pounds would be 5,500 pounds, so 9% would be roughly 5,000 pounds. Those 5,000 pounds of lemons cost $3 per pound, for a total cost of 5,000 × $3 = $15,000. The remaining 17% of lemons is almost twice that weight, or roughly 10,000 pounds. Each pound of these lemons has a corresponding pound of apples, so we can count only the price difference per pound here. Lemons are $1 more per pound, so that's another $10,000, for a total of $15,000 + $10,000 = $25,000. We estimated up on the 17%, so the actual cost should be just a tad under $25,000. That's choice (C).

To see the math, 55,000 × 17% = 9,350 pounds of apples. At $2 per pound, that's 9,350 × $2 = $18,700. 55,000 × 26% = 14,300 pounds of lemons. At $3 per pound, that's 14,300 × $3 = $42,900. The difference in price is $42,900 − $18,700 = $24,200.

Explanation: The G.O.P. Plan

8. Once again the percent calculations look ugly, and once again estimation saves the day: Grapes, oranges, and pears currently make up 9% + 37% + 11% = 57% of the imports. If we double 57% and nix the other two types of fruits, you'd have a bit more than 100%, 18% of which are grapes, so look for a choice that's a bit smaller than 18%. That would be (C).

To see the math, pick 9 for the original number of grapes, 37 for the original number of oranges, and 11 for the original number of pears. That's 9 + 37 + 11 = 57 pieces of fruit. If we double that, we'll have 57 × 2 = 114 pieces of fruit, 18% of which are grapes: $\frac{18}{114} = \frac{3}{19} \approx 15.79\%$.

Ready for more? Try your hand at the following practice problems.

DATA INTERPRETATION PRACTICE SET

Questions 9 and 10 refer to the following table.

Projected Annual Licorice Sales by Volume (in Thousands of Boxes)

Price per box	Licker Us Inc.	Chewy Corp.	Planet Twist
$2.00	3,223	3,455	3,125
$2.25	2,914	3,187	3,076
$2.50	2,564	2,712	2,846
$2.75	1,977	2,109	2,562
$3.00	1,207	1,278	1,413
$3.25	368	412	774

9. If Chewy Corp. sold licorice at $3.00 per box, and Planet Twist sold licorice at $2.50 per box, the number of boxes sold by Chewy Corp. will be approximately what percent of the number of boxes sold by Planet Twist?

(A) 45%

(B) 52%

(C) 79%

(D) 192%

(E) 223%

10. If each company sold licorice at $2.75 per box, which of the following must be true?

   I. Planet Twist sells 453 more boxes than Chewy Corp.
   II. All three companies would have higher gross sales than selling at $3.00 per box.
   III. Licker Us Inc. would have higher gross sales than at any other price point listed.

   (A) I only
   (B) II only
   (C) III only
   (D) I and II
   (E) I, II, and III

Questions 11 and 12 refer to the following table.

Weekly T-Shirt Sales at Local Concerts

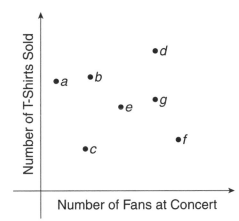

11. In which concert were there fewer T-shirts sold than fans in attendance?

   (A) *a*
   (B) *d*
   (C) *e*
   (D) *f*
   (E) It cannot be determined from the information given.

12. If concert b sold $\frac{3}{7}$ of a T-shirt for every fan in attendance on average, which of the following could have been the number of T-shirts that concert e sold for every fan in attendance?

    (A) $\frac{2}{9}$

    (B) $\frac{1}{2}$

    (C) $\frac{5}{9}$

    (D) $\frac{2}{3}$

    (E) $\frac{9}{11}$

Questions 13–15 refer to the following information.

Roger's Annual Expenditures, 2000–2009 (in Hundreds of Dollars)

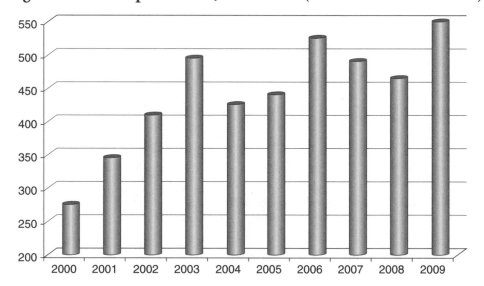

What would YOU do with $5,000.00?

Go to kaptest.com/future

to enter Kaplan's $5,000.00 Brighter Future Sweepstakes!

Kaplan $5,000 Brighter Future Sweepstakes 2009 Complete and Official Rules

1. NO PURCHASE IS NECESSARY TO ENTER OR WIN. A PURCHASE WILL NOT INCREASE YOUR CHANCES OF WINNING.

2. PROMOTION PERIOD. The "Kaplan $5,000 Brighter Future Sweepstakes" ("Sweepstakes") commences at 6:59 A.M. EST on April 1, 2009 and ends at 11:59 P.M. EST on March 31, 2010. Entry forms can be found online at kaptest.com/brighterfuturesweeps. All online entries must be received by March 31, 2010 at 11:59 P.M. EST.

3. ELIGIBILITY. This Sweepstakes is open to legal residents of the 50 United States and the District of Columbia and Canada (excluding the Province of Quebec) who are sixteen (16) years of age or older as of April 1, 2009. Officers, directors, representatives and employees of Kaplan (from here on called "Sponsor"), its parent, affiliates or subsidiaries, or their respective advertising, promotion, publicity, production, and judging agencies and their immediate families and household members are not eligible to enter.

4. TO ENTER. To enter simply go to kaptest.com/brighterfuturesweeps and fill-out the online entry form between April 1, 2009 and March 31, 2010.

As part of your entry, you will be asked to provide your first and last name, email address, permanent address and phone number, parent or legal guardian name if under eighteen (18), and the name of your undergraduate school.

LIMIT ONE ENTRY PER PERSON AND EMAIL ADDRESS. Multiple entries will be disqualified. Entries are void if they contain typographical, printing or other errors. Entries generated by a script, macro or other automated means are void. Entries that are mutilated, altered, incomplete, mechanically reproduced, tampered with, illegible, inaccurate, forged, irregular in any way, or otherwise not in compliance with these Official Rules are also void. All entries become the property of the Sponsor and will not be returned to the entrant. Sponsor and those working on its behalf will not be responsible for lost, late, misdirected or damaged mail or email or for Internet, network, computer hardware and software, phone or other technical errors, malfunctions and delays that may occur. Entries will be deemed to have been submitted by the authorized account holder of the email account from which the entry is made. The authorized account holder is the natural person to whom an email address is assigned by an Internet access provider, online service provider or other organization (e.g. business, educational institution, etc.) responsible for assigning email addresses for the domain associated with the submitted email address. By entering or accepting a prize in this Sweepstakes, entrants agree to be bound by the decisions of the judges, the Sponsor and these Official Rules and to comply with all applicable federal, state and local laws and regulations. Odds of winning depend on the number of eligible entries received.

5. WINNER SELECTION. Two (2) winners will be selected for the First Prize; two (2) winners for the Second Prize, five (5) winners for the Third Prize, five (5) winners for Fourth Prize, five (5) winners for the Fifth Prize, and 25 winners for the Sixth Prize from all eligible entries received in a random drawing to be held on or about May 11, 2010. The drawing will be conducted by an independent judge whose decisions shall be final and binding in all regards. Participants need not be present to win. Please note that if the entrant selected as the winner resides in Canada, he/she will have to correctly answer a timed, test-prep question in order to be confirmed as the winner and claim the prize.

6. WINNER NOTIFICATION AND VALIDATION. Winners of the drawing will be notified by mail within 10 days after the drawing. An Affidavit of Eligibility and Compliance with these Official Rules and a Liability and (unless prohibited) Publicity Release must be executed and returned by the potential winner within twenty-one (21) days after prize notification is sent. If the winner is under eighteen (18) years of age, the prize will be awarded to the winner's parent or legal guardian who will be required to execute an affidavit. Failure of the potential winner to complete, sign and return any requested documents within such period or the return of any prize notification or prize as undeliverable may result in disqualification and selection of an alternate winner in Sponsor's sole discretion. You are not a winner unless your submissions are validated.

In the event that a winner chooses not to accept his or her prize, does not respond to winner notification within the time period noted on the notification or does not return a completed Affidavit of Eligibility and Compliance with these Official Rules and a Liability and (unless prohibited) Publicity Release within twenty-one (21) days after prize notification is sent, the prize may be forfeited and an alternate winner selected in Sponsor's sole discretion.

7. PRIZES.

• First Prize: Two (2) winners will be selected to win $5,000.00 USD.

• Second Prize: Two (2) winners will be selected to win $1,000.00 USD.

• Third Prize: Five (5) winners will be selected to win their choice of a Free Kaplan SAT, ACT, GMAT, GRE, LSAT, MCAT, DAT, OAT, or PCAT Classroom Course (retail value up to $1,899).

• Fourth Prize: Five (5) winners will be selected to win their choice of Ten (10) Free Hours of GMAT, GRE, LSAT, MCAT, DAT, OAT, PCAT Private Tutoring (retail value of $1,500), or Ten (10) Free Hours of SAT, ACT, PSAT Premier Tutoring (retail value of $2,000).

• Fifth Prize: Five (5) winners will be selected to win their choice of Three (3) Free Hours of Admissions Consulting for Precollege (retail value of $450) or three (3) Free Hours of Business School, Law School, Grad School or Med School Admissions Consulting (retail value of $729).

• Sixth Prize: Twenty-five (25) winners will be selected to win $100.00 USD.

For winners of the Third and Fourth Prizes, the winner must redeem the course at Kaplan locations in the US offering them and have completed the program before December 31, 2012.

Prizes are not transferable. No substitution of prizes for cash or other goods and services is permitted, except Sponsor reserves the right in its sole discretion to substitute any prize with a prize of comparable value. Any applicable taxes or fees are the winner's sole responsibility. All prizes must be redeemed within 21 days of notice of award and course prizes used by December 31, 2012.

8. GENERAL CONDITIONS. By entering the Sweepstakes or accepting the Sweepstakes prize, winner accepts all the conditions, restrictions, requirements and/or regulations required by the Sponsor in connection with the Sweepstakes. Unless otherwise prohibited by law, acceptance of a prize constitutes permission to use winner's name, picture, likeness, address (city and state) and biographical information for advertising and publicity purposes for this and/or similar promotions, without prior approval or compensation. Acceptance of a prize constitutes a waiver of any claim to royalties, rights or remuneration for said use. Winner agrees to release and hold harmless the Sponsor, its parent, affiliates and subsidiaries, and each of their respective directors, officers, employees, agents, and successors from any and all claims, damages, injury, death, loss or other liability that may arise from winner's participation in the Sweepstakes or the awarding, acceptance, possession, use or misuse of the prize. Sponsor reserves the right in its sole discretion to modify or cancel all or any portions of the Sweepstakes because of technical errors or malfunctions, viruses, hackers, or for other reasons beyond Sponsor's control that impair or corrupt the Sweepstakes in any manner. In such event, Sponsor shall award prizes at random from among the eligible entries received up to the time of the impairment or corruption. Sponsor also reserves the right in its sole discretion to disqualify any entrant who fails to comply with these Official Rules, who attempts to enter the Sweepstakes in any manner or through any means other than as described in these Official Rules, or who attempts to disrupt the Sweepstakes or the kaptest.com website or to circumvent any of these Official Rules.

9. WINNERS' LIST. Starting August 15, 2010, a winners' list may be obtained by sending a self-addressed, stamped envelope to: "$5,000 Kaplan Brighter Future Sweepstakes" Winners' List, Kaplan Test Prep and Admissions Marketing Department, 1440 Broadway, 8th Floor New York, NY 10018. All winners' list requests must be received by December 1, 2010.

10. USE OF ENTRANT AND WINNER INFORMATION. The information that you provide in connection with the Sweepstakes may be used for Sponsor's and select Corporate Partners' purposes to send you information about Sponsor's and its Corporate Partners' products and services. If you would like your name removed from Sponsor's mailing list or if you do not wish to receive information from Sponsor or its Corporate Partners, write to:

Direct Marketing Department
Attn: Kaplan Brighter Future Sweepstakes Opt Out
1440 Broadway
8th Floor
New York NY 10018

11. SPONSOR. The Sponsor of this Sweepstakes is: Kaplan Test Prep and Admissions and Kaplan Publishing, 1440 Broadway, 8th Floor New York, NY 10018.

12. THIS SWEEPSTAKES IS VOID WHERE PROHIBITED, TAXED OR OTHERWISE RESTRICTED BY LAW.

All trademarks are the property of their respective owner.

Roger's Annual Expenditures, 2006–2008

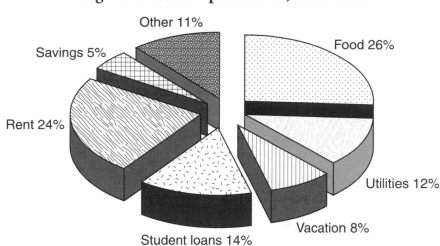

13. Between which two years did Roger's annual expenditures double?

    (A) 2000 and 2001
    (B) 2001 and 2004
    (C) 2000 and 2009
    (D) 2002 and 2006
    (E) 2003 and 2005

14. Approximately how much more money did Roger save in 2006 than 2008?

    (A) $3
    (B) $6
    (C) $125
    (D) $300
    (E) $750

15. Having stuck to a responsible budget, Roger is able to pay off the last of his student loans in 2009, eliminating this category from future budgets. If his expenditures total $60,000 in 2010, and they proportionally follow the same breakdown as the 2006–2008 period, approximately how much did Roger spend on vacations in 2010?

    (A) $4,800
    (B) $5,235
    (C) $5,580
    (D) $6,000
    (E) $6,760

Questions 16–20 are based on the following graphs.

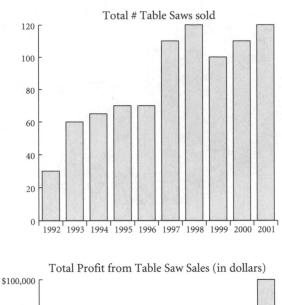

Total # Table Saws sold

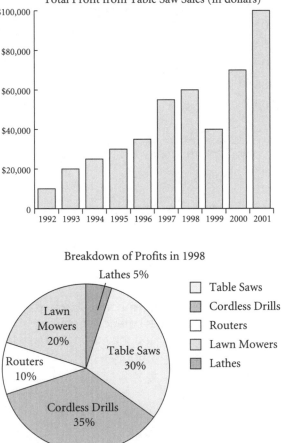

Total Profit from Table Saw Sales (in dollars)

Breakdown of Profits in 1998

16. In 1998, what were the total profits from sales of all the hardware tools?

    (A) $200,000
    (B) $250,000
    (C) $300,000
    (D) $350,000
    (E) $400,000

17. Which year had the greatest percentage increase in number of table saws sold from the previous year?

    (A) 1993
    (B) 1995
    (C) 1997
    (D) 2000
    (E) 2001

18. Of the following, what is the closest to the percentage change in profits from table saws between 1998 and 1999?

    (A) A 50% increase
    (B) A 33% increase
    (C) A 17% decrease
    (D) A 33% decrease
    (E) A 50% decrease

19. If the fixed cost of manufacturing table saws in 1993 was $22,000, how much did each table saw sell for?

    (A) $300
    (B) $450
    (C) $500
    (D) $600
    (E) $700

20. In 1998, what were the approximate profits from the sales of cordless drills?

    (A) $50,000
    (B) $70,000
    (C) $80,000
    (D) $90,000
    (E) $100,000

DATA INTERPRETATION PRACTICE SET ANSWER KEY

9.	A	15.	C
10.	B	16.	A
11.	E	17.	A
12.	A	18.	D
13.	C	19.	E
14.	D	20.	B

EXPLANATIONS

9. With all the different values, make sure that you are looking up the correct columns. With percentage, the fact that the licorice sold is in thousands of boxes doesn't matter, so we can ignore that for this question. The numbers are ugly, so estimate: Chewy Corp. sells 1,278 at $3.00 per box while Planet Twist sells 2,846 at $2.50 per box. Since 1,278 is a bit less than half of 2,846, the only choice that works is (A).

10. With any Roman numeral question, the first step should be to look at the choices. In this question, statements I and II show up three times each, while III shows up only twice, so begin by checking the first two statements:

    I. You might have been tempted to say this is true, but this is the oldest trick in the book. The heading above the table tells you that the numbers are given in thousands of boxes, so I is false. Eliminate (A), (D), and (E).

    II. At $3.00, a mere $0.25 more per box, each of the three companies sheds nearly half of its sales volume, so estimation alone should be enough to see that this statement is true. That makes (B) correct, and there's no need to check statement III.

    III. For the curious: estimation can also make quick work of this one by comparing Licker Us Inc.'s sales at $2.75 to their sales at $2.00. Ignoring the fact that boxes are listed in thousands for a moment (as that won't affect the outcome), at $2.75, you have "less than $3.00" times "less than 2,000," or "less than $6,000" total, whereas at $2.00, you have "$2.00" times "more than 3,000," or "more than $6,000" total. Therefore, $2.75 clearly does not lead to the highest gross sales for Licker Us.

11. While the graph seems rather simple, be sure to take the time to get familiar with it. Doing so would reveal that (D) is a trap choice, as the axes on this graph do not have a scale printed. Without this information, there is no way of knowing whether any of the concerts had fewer T-shirts sold than fans in attendance, so (E) is correct.

12. While the graph does not provide absolute numbers, you won't need them to answer this question. e is lower than b and farther to the right, so more total people bought fewer total T-shirts. Concert b sold an average of $\frac{3}{7}$ of a T-shirt per fan, so concert e would've sold *fewer* than $\frac{3}{7}$ of a T-shirt per fan. The only choice that works is (A).

13. The question seems innocent enough, but watch the scale. Since the scale does not start at 0, you cannot simply eyeball the chart to answer this question. Roger's expenses in 2000 were around the 275 mark, and his expenses in 2009 were around the 550 mark, so (C) is correct. No other pair of years even comes close to doubling.

14. The choices are spaced far apart, so estimate. According to the chart, Roger's 2006 expenditures were roughly at the 525 mark, while his 2008 expenditures were roughly at the 460 mark. 5% of 525 ≈ 26, and 5% of 460 ≈ 23, so he saved ≈ 26 − 23 = 3 more. The chart is in hundreds of dollars, so Roger saved about $300 more in 2006. That's (D).

15. With the student loan category eliminated, each other category would be a bit larger on a percentage basis. Vacations from 2006 to 2008 are 8 out of 100, or 8%. With student loans eliminated in 2010, it would be 8 out of $100 - 14 = 86$, or a bit more than 9%. 9% of $60,000 is $5,400, and 10% of $60,000 is $6,000, so the answer must be between those two figures. That makes (C) correct.

16. From the second bar graph, the profits from table saws in 1998 were about $60,000. From the pie chart, table saws were 30% of the total profits. Let's call the total profits T dollars. Then 30% of T dollars is $60,000. So $0.3T = 60,000$, and $T = 60,000/3 = 60,000 \times \dfrac{10}{10} \times \dfrac{1}{.03} \times 10 = 600,000/3 = 200,000$. That's (A).

17. The year with the biggest percent increase over the previous year will be the year where the increase is the biggest fraction of the amount in the previous year. We see that in 1993, the increase from 1992 was approximately $60 - 30$, or 30. This is approximately a 100 percent increase, and the greatest per cent increase over the previous year among all the years from 1993 through 2001. There was a greater increase from 1996 to 1997 than from 1992 to 1993. The increase from 1996 to 1997 was about $110 - 70 = 40$. However, the per cent increase from 1996 to 1997 is approximately $\dfrac{40}{70} \times 100\%$, which is less than 100%. That's (A).

18. In 1998, the profits from table saws were approximately $60,000. In 1999, the profits from table saws were approximately $40,000. From 1998 to 1999 there was a decrease in the profits from table saws. In general,

    $$\text{Percent decrease} = \frac{\text{Original value} - \text{New value}}{\text{Original value}} \times 100\%.$$

    Here, the percent decrease is approximately $\dfrac{\$60,000 - \$40,000}{\$60,000} \times 100\%$

    $$= \frac{\$20,000}{\$60,000} \times 100\% = \frac{1}{3} \times 100\%$$

    A percent decrease of $33\dfrac{1}{3}\%$ is closest to (D).

19. In 1993, the profits were $20,000. Using the formula Profit = Revenue − Cost, we have that Revenue = Cost + Profit. The cost was $22,000. So the revenue was $22,000 + $20,000 = $42,000. Since in 1993, 60 table saws were sold, each table saw was sold for $\dfrac{\$42,000}{60}$ which is $700 (E).

20. In 1998, the profits from table saws were about $60,000 and this profit is 30% of the total profits. Let's call the total call the total profits T dollars. Then 30% of T dollars is $60,000. So $0.3T = 60,000/0.3 = 60,000 \times 10/0.3 \times 10 = 200,000$.

    The total profits in 1998 were approximately $200,000. The profits from cordless drills were 35% of the total. So the profits from cordless drills were approximately 0.35($200,00), which is $70,000 (B).

CHAPTER EIGHT

Numeric Entry

The brand-new question type from ETS. The one that puts the "math" back into the Quantitative section. Many GRE test takers believe that there can be no strategy—no "tricks"—to Numeric Entry. After all, if there are no answer choices to choose from, then these can't be any different from the problems on a normal math test, right?

The advanced test taker in you may have been suspicious. You may have wondered whether there really is a question type on the GRE that would be "pure math"—devoid of critical thinking. You would be right to wonder. For even when ETS omits answer choices, the GRE's first and foremost goal is still to test your critical thinking. Leaving out the answer choices simply makes it harder for the average test taker to notice that.

Numeric Entry is one of ETS's greatest attempts at trying to convince examinees that the Quantitative section is simply a math test—one that takes time and can lead to mathematical errors in calculation. But with Kaplan's proven strategies, you will pierce this illusion. Practice well and Numeric Entry will not sway you from your critical thinking crusade to a perfect 800.

THE INSTRUCTIONS

Numeric Entry problems resemble word problems in all aspects except one—instead of five answer choices, you are presented with a box in which to type your answer. You may input numbers, decimal points (period), and minus signs (hyphen). If an answer calls for a symbol, such as $, %, or °, it will already be provided to you next to the box. Questions that call for a fractional answer will provide two boxes, one each for the numerator and denominator. You may not use decimal points in fractions, and your answer does not need to be reduced to lowest terms.

Every official GRE CAT administered during the trial period, which began in November 2007 and is still ongoing at the time of this publication, will include either one Numeric Entry question or none at all. Numeric Entry questions will remain unscored until ETS feels that it has gathered enough data, at which point they will be added to the normal GRE lineup. Since only ETS knows when that is, it is best to treat this as a scored question type during your preparation.

KAPLAN'S 3-STEP METHOD FOR NUMERIC ENTRY

Step 1: Read through the question carefully.

With no choices, you'll *really* want to be sure that you understood the question.

Step 2: Choose your approach.

For many Numeric Entry problems, the straight math is *not* your only choice!

Step 3: Ensure that you answered the right question before submitting your answer.

No choices can also mean solving for the wrong thing and not noticing, so check!

Numeric Entry Practice Set

1. If z is the product of four distinct prime factors, how many of z's factors are not prime?

   Click on the answer box and then type in a number.

   Use backspace to erase.

2. In a glass jar, three of the eight lottery tickets are winning tickets. If Ruth buys three tickets, what is the probability that all three of them are winning tickets?

   Type in your answer as a fraction.

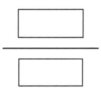

   Click on each answer box and then type in a number.

   Use backspace to erase.

3. On Monday afternoon, *ABC* stock closes 25% below its opening price. On Tuesday afternoon, *ABC* stock closes 20% below Monday's closing price. On Wednesday afternoon, *ABC* stock closes 25% above Tuesday's closing price. If, on Thursday afternoon, *ABC* stock closes at Monday's opening price, what percent above Wednesday's closing price did it close at?

   Type in your answer to the <u>nearest tenth of a percent</u>.

 %

   Click on the answer box and then type in a number.

   Use backspace to erase.

ARITHMETIC

Questions 4–9

4. What is the smallest multiple of 20, 24, and 28?

Click on the answer box and then type in a number.
Use backspace to erase.

5. The average (arithmetic mean) of 38 numbers is 50. When two new numbers are added, the new average is 52. If one of the new numbers is 60, what is the other number?

Click on the answer box and then type in a number.
Use backspace to erase.

6. A recipe for honey lemon tea calls for honey, lemon, and water to be added in the ratio 6:10:14, respectively. If 10 ounces of honey are used in a bottle of this tea, how many ounces of tea are in the bottle?

 ounces

Click on the answer box and then type in a number.
Use backspace to erase.

7. For her son's birthday party, Sandra is baking 60 cupcakes. She made 24 cupcakes with frosting and 26 cupcakes with sprinkles. If Sandra made 16 cupcakes with both frosting and sprinkles, how many cupcakes had neither frosting nor sprinkles?

Click on the answer box and then type in a number.
Use backspace to erase.

8. Miranda's bathtub has a gold faucet, a silver faucet, and a rusted faucet. Working alone, the gold faucet takes 20 minutes to fill the tub, the silver faucet takes 40 minutes, and the rusted faucet takes a full hour. If Miranda fills the tub using all three faucets, what fraction of the water came from the rusted faucet?

   Type in your answer as a fraction.

   Click on each answer box and then type in a number.

   Use backspace to erase.

9. On her way to work, Judy drives 20 miles at 60 miles per hour before narrowly missing a deer. A bit frazzled, she reduces her speed to 30 miles per hour for the remainder of her trip. If the whole trip was 80 miles long, how many more minutes did it take her than if she had driven the entire distance at 40 miles per hour?

   [   ] minutes

   Click on the answer box and then type in a number.

   Use backspace to erase.

ALGEBRA

Questions 10–12

10. If $15z - 6y - 7x = 23$ and $7x + 9y - 12z = 10$, what is the value of $y + z$?

    $y + z =$ [   ]

    Click on the answer box and then type in a number.

    Use backspace to erase.

11. It cost 24 people a total of $120 to gain admission to the local amusement park. If adult tickets are $7 and child tickets are $4, how many of the 24 people were children?

    [   ]

    Click on the answer box and then type in a number.

    Use backspace to erase.

12. For all integers a and b, $b < 0 < a$ and $a + b < 5$. If $b > -15$, what is the greatest possible value of $a - b$?

Click on the answer box and then type in a number.
Use backspace to erase.

GEOMETRY

Questions 13–15

13. If square X has a diagonal of $9\sqrt{2}$ inches and square Y has a side of $9\sqrt{2}$ inches, then square X's area is what percent of square Y's?

%

Click on the answer box and then type in a number.
Use backspace to erase.

14. To train for a marathon, Mitch ran nine miles north, five miles west, and another three miles north. If he had instead run directly from start to finish in a straight line, how many miles shorter would his run have been?

miles

Click on the answer box and then type in a number.
Use backspace to erase.

15. A certain rectangle has an area of 288. What is the greatest possible perimeter for this rectangle if both its length and width are integers?

Click on the answer box and then type in a number.
Use backspace to erase.

NUMERIC ENTRY PRACTICE SET ANSWER KEY

1. 12
2. $\dfrac{1}{56}$
3. 33.3
4. 840
5. 120
6. 50
7. 26
8. $\dfrac{2}{11}$

9. 20
10. 11
11. 16
12. 32
13. 50
14. 4
15. 578

EXPLANATIONS

1. While there aren't any answer choices to work with, variables in the question stem should still prompt you to pick numbers. You're told that z is the product of four distinct primes, so pick the four smallest primes to test: 2, 3, 5, and 7. $2 \times 3 \times 5 \times 7 = 210$, so 210 is one possible value for z. How many factors does 210 have? The easiest way to figure that out without forgetting any of them is to start with 1 and 210 on opposite ends, then work your way toward the center:

1	210
1, 2	105, 210
1, 2, 3	70, 105, 210
1, 2, 3, 5	42, 70, 105, 210
1, 2, 3, 5, 6	35, 42, 70, 105, 210
1, 2, 3, 5, 6, 7	30, 35, 42, 70, 105, 210
1, 2, 3, 5, 6, 7, 10	21, 30, 35, 42, 70, 105, 210

   1, 2, 3, 5, 6, 7, 10, 14, 15, 21, 30, 35, 42, 70, 105, 210

   So 210 has 16 factors. Be sure not to stop too soon, as that is *not* what the question is asking for. Four of the factors are prime (the four mentioned in the question stem), so z has $16 - 4 = 12$ factors that aren't prime. Type in **12** as your answer.

2. Ruth is interested in only winners (aren't we all?), and you're here to figure out her chances. With three winners out of eight, the probability that Ruth's first purchase will net a winner is $\frac{3}{8}$. After buying her first winning ticket, there are two winners out of seven tickets left, so the probability of picking the second winner is $\frac{2}{7}$. With one winner to go out of six remaining tickets, the probability of snagging the last winner on the third purchase is $\frac{1}{6}$. To find the probability of all of that happening, multiply the three probabilities: $\frac{3}{8} \times \frac{2}{7} \times \frac{1}{6} = \frac{1}{56}$. **Type 1 in the numerator and 56 in the denominator.**

3. The problem presents a seriously volatile stock with no actual amounts, so pick numbers. Since we're dealing with percents, pick $100 as the original price of *ABC* stock. On Monday afternoon, it dips 25% to $100 - 100(.25) = 100 - 25 = 75$. On Tuesday afternoon, it dips a further 20% to $75 - 75(.2) = 75 - 15 = 60$. On Wednesday it recovers 25% to $60 + 60(.25) = 60 + 15 = 75$. At this point, we are $100 - 75 = 25$ below the original price. To close at Monday's opening price on Thursday afternoon, *ABC* stock would need to increase $\frac{\$25}{\$75} = \frac{1}{3} = 33.3\%$. **Type 33.3 into the box.**

   Think you've got the hang of this wacky new format? See how you do with the following.

4. The math looks ugly, so don't do it the straight math way. The key to this problem is prime factorization: $20 = 2 \times 2 \times 5$, $24 = 2 \times 2 \times 2 \times 3$, and $28 = 2 \times 2 \times 7$. So the smallest multiple of these three numbers must include three 2s, one 3, one 5, and one 7. That would be $2 \times 2 \times 2 \times 3 \times 5 \times 7 = 840$. **Type 840 into the box.**

5. If the average of 38 numbers is 50, their sum is $38 \times 50 = 1,900$. Adding two new numbers raises the average to 52, so the new sum is $40 \times 52 = 2,080$, and the two new numbers have a sum of $2,080 - 1,900 = 180$. One of them is 60, so the other number is $180 - 60 = 120$. **Type 120 into the box.**

6. Here is a classic example of why you shouldn't read a question too quickly. The ratio is 6:10:14, but the 10 ounces given are of *honey*, which corresponds to the 6 in the ratio. With 6 ounces of honey, you would have $6 + 10 + 14 = 30$ ounces of tea, so the ratio of honey to tea is 6:30, or 1:5. With 10 ounces of honey, you would have $10 \times 5 = 50$ ounces of tea. **Type 50 into the box.**

7. Sandra made 24 cupcakes with frosting and 26 with sprinkles, for a total of $24 + 26 = 50$ cupcakes with one or the other. Sixteen of the 60 cupcakes had both frosting and sprinkles, so 16 of the 50 were counted twice. That means $50 - 16 = 34$ cupcakes had either frosting, sprinkles, or both, and $60 - 34 = 26$ cupcakes had neither. **Type 26 into the box.**

8. Miranda's multiple faucets can be quite difficult to figure out with only one bathtub, so let's try looking at it a different way. Suppose all three faucets were running for 120 minutes. In that amount of time, the gold faucet would fill $120 \div 20 = 6$ tubs, the silver faucet would fill $120 \div 40 = 3$ tubs, and the rusted faucet would fill $120 \div 60 = 2$ tubs. That's a total of $6 + 3 + 2 = 11$ tubs filled in the 120 minutes, two of which were filled by the rusted faucet. How does this help? Well, the actual amount of time elapsed does not affect the rate of work, so the rusted faucet will always fill 2 out of every 11 tubs that the trio fills together. So in Miranda's case, $\dfrac{2}{11}$ of the water came from the rusted faucet. **Type 2 in the numerator and 11 in the denominator.**

9. Poor Judy is wondering how much longer the reckless driving made her trip. To figure that out, you'll need to find the amount of time she actually spent. Since the final answer will be in minutes, let's tally up the time in minutes as well. She drove the first 20 miles at 60 mph, so that leg of the trip took 20 minutes. The remainder of her 80-mile trip would be $80 - 20 = 60$ miles, which she drove at 30 mph, so that part took two hours = 120 minutes. That's a total of 140 minutes. Had she driven the entire course at a constant 40 mph, it would've taken her two hours to drive 80 miles, or 120 minutes. Therefore, it took her $140 - 120 = 20$ additional minutes. **Type 20 into the box.**

10. When a GRE problem asks for the value of an expression, such as $y + z$, it will usually be impossible to find the value for the individual variables. To solve this problem, rearrange the variables to match, then combine:

$$
\begin{array}{r}
7x + 9y - 12z = 10 \\
-7x - 6y + 15z = 23 \\
\hline
3y + 3z = 33 \\
3(y + z) = 33 \\
y + z = 11
\end{array}
$$

Type 11 into the box.

11. As a word problem, this would be a great one to back-solve. Unfortunately, with no choices in Numeric Entry, you are forced to do the algebra. Let a = the number of adult tickets and c = the number of child tickets. This gives us two equations: $7a + 4c = 120$ and $a + c = 24$. Combine to solve for c:

$$7a + 4c = 120$$
$$\underline{-7(a + c = 24)}$$
$$-3c = -48$$
$$c = 16$$

Type 16 into the box.

12. There's a lot going on here, so the key is to begin with the most concrete element of the problem. In this case, that would be the fact that a is positive and b is negative, meaning the expression $a - b$ will be at its greatest when the absolute values of a and b are both at their greatest. Since $b > -15$, b is -14. That means $a + (-14) < 5$ and $a < 19$, so $a = 18$ and the greatest value for $a - b = 18 - (-14) = 18 + 14 = 32$. **Type 32 into the box.**

13. A square's diagonal divides it into two identical isosceles right triangles whose sides are in the proportion $x:x:x\sqrt{2}$. Square X has a diagonal of $9\sqrt{2}$ inches, so it must have a side of 9 inches and an area of 9 inches $\times$ 9 inches = 81 sq. inches. Square Y has a side of $9\sqrt{2}$ inches, so its area is $9\sqrt{2}$ inches $\times$ $9\sqrt{2}$ inches = 162 sq. inches. Since 81 is half of 162, square X's area is 50% of square Y's. **Type 50 into the box.**

14. Since the problem does not provide a diagram, draw your own to better visualize it:

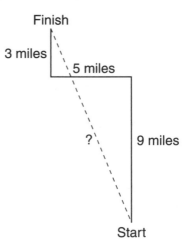

Doesn't seem too helpful yet, but if you add the following lines

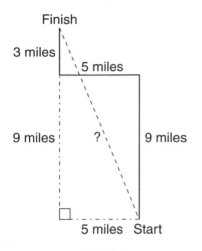

it becomes a 5-12-13 right triangle with legs 5 and 12, so the distance from start to finish is 13. Mitch ran a total of $9 + 5 + 3 = 17$ miles, so his actual trip is $17 - 13 = 4$ miles longer. **Type 4 into the box.**

15. The perimeter of a rectangle is the sum of its sides, and the area is length × width, so the rectangle's perimeter will be greatest when its length and width correspond to the factor pair of 288 that has the greatest sum. You *could* list all the factors of 288, but that could take a while. Instead, let's examine the first few pairs of factors: $1 \times 288 = 288$, $2 \times 144 = 288$, $3 \times 96 = 288$. Since the sum keeps shrinking as we go, the greatest perimeter will be when the length and width are 1 and 288 (not necessarily in that order). A 1×288 rectangle has a perimeter of $1 + 1 + 288 + 288 = 578$. **Type 578 into the box.**

section three

GRE RESOURCES

CHAPTER NINE

The 100 Most Important Math Concepts

The math on the GRE covers a lot of ground—from basic algebra to symbol problems to geometry. Don't let yourself be intimidated.

We've highlighted the 100 most important concepts that you need to remember and divided them into three levels. The GRE Quantitative section tests your understanding of a relatively limited number of mathematical concepts, all of which you will be able to learn.

Level 1 is the most basic. You can't answer any GRE math questions if you don't know Level 1 math. Most people preparing to take the GRE are already pretty good at Level 1 math, but look over the Level 1 list just to make sure you're comfortable with the basics.

Level 2 where most people start their review of math. Level 2 skills and formulas come into play quite frequently on the GRE, especially in the medium and hard questions.

Level 3 is the hardest math you'll find on the GRE. Don't spend a lot of time on Level 3 if you still have gaps in Level 2; but once you've mastered Level 2, tackling Level 3 can put you over the top, and send you well on your way to that 800 on the Quantitative section.

LEVEL 1 (MATH YOU ALREADY KNOW)

1. How to add, subtract, multiply, and divide WHOLE NUMBERS

2. How to add, subtract, multiply, and divide FRACTIONS

3. How to add, subtract, multiply, and divide DECIMALS

4. How to convert FRACTIONS TO DECIMALS and DECIMALS TO FRACTIONS

5. How to add, subtract, multiply, and divide POSITIVE AND NEGATIVE NUMBERS

6. How to plot points on the NUMBER LINE

7. How to plug a number into an ALGEBRAIC EXPRESSION

8. How to SOLVE a simple EQUATION

9. How to add and subtract LINE SEGMENTS

10. How to find the THIRD ANGLE of a TRIANGLE, given the other two angles

LEVEL 2 (MATH YOU MIGHT NEED TO REVIEW)

11. How to use PEMDAS

When you're given an ugly arithmetic expression, it's important to know the order of operations. Just remember PEMDAS (as in "Please Excuse My Dear Aunt Sally"). What PEMDAS means is this: clean up **Parentheses** first; then deal with **Exponents**; then do the **Multiplication** and **Division** together, going from left to right; and finally do the **Addition** and **Subtraction** together, again going from left to right.

Example:

$$9 - 2 \times (5 - 3)^2 + 6 \div 3 =$$

Begin with the parentheses:

$$9 - 2 \times (2)^2 + 6 \div 3$$

Then do the exponent:

$$9 - 2 \times 4 + 6 \div 3$$

Now do multiplication and division from left to right:

$$9 - 8 + 2$$

Finally, do addition and subtraction from left to right:

$$9 - 8 + 2 = 1 + 2 = 3$$

12. How to use the PERCENT FORMULA

Identify the part, the percent, and the whole.

$$Part = percent \times whole$$

Find the part.

Example: What is 12 percent of 25?

Setup: $Part = \dfrac{12}{100} \times 25 = 3$

Find the percent.

Example: 45 is what percent of 9?

Setup: $45 = Percent \times 9$

$$Percent = \dfrac{45}{9} = 5 = 5 \times 100\% = 500\%$$

Find the whole.

Example: 15 is $\dfrac{3}{5}$ percent of what number?

Setup: $15 = \dfrac{3}{5}\left(\dfrac{1}{100}\right) \times whole$

$$15 = \dfrac{3}{500} \times whole$$

$$whole = 15\left(\dfrac{500}{3}\right) = 5(500) = 2{,}500$$

13. How to use the PERCENT INCREASE/DECREASE FORMULAS

Identify the original whole and the amount of increase/decrease.

$$Percent\ increase = \frac{amount\ of\ increase}{original\ whole} \times 100\%$$

$$Percent\ decrease = \frac{amount\ of\ decrease}{original\ whole} \times 100\%$$

Example: The price goes up from $80 to $100. What is the percent increase?

Setup: $Percent\ increase = \dfrac{20}{80} \times 100\% = 25\%$

14. How to predict whether a sum, difference, or product will be ODD or EVEN

Don't bother memorizing the rules. Just take simple numbers like 1 and 2 and see what happens.

Example: If m is even and n is odd, is the product mn odd or even?

Setup: Say $m = 2$ and $n = 1$.

2×1 is even, so mn is even.

15. How to recognize MULTIPLES OF 2, 3, 4, 5, 6, 9, 10, and 12

  2: Last digit is even

  3: Sum of digits is a multiple of 3

  4: Last two digits are a multiple of 4

  5: Last digit is 5 or 0

  6: Sum of digits is a multiple of 3 and last digit is even

  9: Sum of digits is a multiple of 9

10: Last digit is 0

12: Sum of digits is a multiple of 3 and last two digits are a multiple of 4

16. How to find a COMMON FACTOR

Break both numbers down to their prime factors to see what they have in common. Then multiply the shared prime factors to find all common factors.

  Example: What factors greater than 1 do 135 and 225 have in common?

  Setup: First, find the prime factors of 135 and 225; $135 = 3 \times 3 \times 3 \times 5$, and $225 = 3 \times 3 \times 5 \times 5$. The numbers share $3 \times 3 \times 5$ in common. Thus, aside from 3 and 5, the remaining common factors can be found by multiplying 3, 3, and 5 in every possible combination: $3 \times 3 = 9$, $3 \times 5 = 15$, and $3 \times 3 \times 5 = 45$.

17. How to find a COMMON MULTIPLE

The product is the easiest common multiple to find. If the two numbers have any factors in common, you can divide them out of the product to get a lower common multiple.

  Example: What is the least common multiple of 28 and 42?

  Setup: The product of $28 \times 42 = 1,176$ is a common multiple, but not the least. $28 = 2 \times 2 \times 7$, and $42 = 2 \times 3 \times 7$. They share a 2 and a 7, so divide the product by 2 and then by 7. $1,176 \div 2 = 588$. $588 \div 7 = 84$. The least common multiple is 84.

18. How to find the AVERAGE

$$Average = \frac{Sum\ of\ terms}{Number\ of\ terms}$$

  Example: What is the average of 3, 4, and 8?

  Setup: $Average = \dfrac{3+4+8}{3} = \dfrac{15}{3} = 5$

19. How to use the AVERAGE to find the SUM

$$Sum = (Average) \times (Number\ of\ terms)$$

  Example: 17.5 is the average (arithmetic mean) of 24 numbers. What is the sum?

  Setup: $Sum = 17.5 \times 24 = 420$

20. How to find the AVERAGE of CONSECUTIVE NUMBERS

The average of evenly spaced numbers is simply the average of the smallest number and the largest number. The average of all the integers from 13 to 77, for example, is the same as the average of 13 and 77:

$$\frac{13 + 77}{2} = \frac{90}{2} = 45$$

21. How to COUNT CONSECUTIVE NUMBERS

The number of integers from A to B inclusive is $B - A + 1$.

   Example: How many integers are there from 73 through 419, inclusive?

   Setup: $419 - 73 + 1 = 347$

22. How to find the SUM OF CONSECUTIVE NUMBERS

   Sum = (*Average*) × (*Number of terms*)

   Example: What is the sum of the integers from 10 through 50, inclusive?

   Setup: Average = (10 + 50) ÷ 2 = 30, Number of terms = 50 − 10 + 1 = 41, Sum = 30 × 41 = 1,230

23. How to find the MEDIAN

Put the numbers in numerical order and take the middle number. (If there's an even number of numbers, the average of the two numbers in the middle is the median.)

   Example: What is the median of 88, 86, 57, 94, and 73?

   Setup: Put the numbers in numerical order and take the middle number:

      57, 73, 86, 88, 94

The median is 86. (If there's an even number of numbers, take the average of the two in the middle.)

24. How to find the MODE

Take the number that appears most often. For example, if your test scores were 88, 57, 68, 85, 98, 93, 93, 84, and 81, the mode of the scores is 93 because it appears more often than any other score. (If there's a tie for most often, then there's more than one mode.)

25. How to find the RANGE

Simply take the positive difference between the highest and lowest values. Using the previous example, if your test scores were 88, 57, 68, 85, 98, 93, 93, 84, and 81, the range of the scores is 41, the highest value minus the lowest value (98 − 57 = 41).

26. How to use actual numbers to determine a RATIO

To find a ratio, put the number associated with *of* on the top and the word associated with *to* on the bottom.

$$Ratio = \frac{of}{to}$$

The ratio of 20 oranges to 12 apples is $\dfrac{20}{12}$, or $\dfrac{5}{3}$.

27. How to use a ratio to determine an ACTUAL NUMBER

Set up a proportion.

Example: The ratio of boys to girls is 3 to 4. If there are 135 boys, how many girls are there?

Setup: $\dfrac{3}{4} = \dfrac{135}{x}$

$3 \times x = 4 \times 135$

$x = 180$

28. How to use actual numbers to determine a RATE

Identify the quantities and the units to be compared. Keep the units straight.

Example: Anders typed 9,450 words in $3\dfrac{1}{2}$ hours. What was his rate in words per minute?

Setup: First convert $3\dfrac{1}{2}$ hours to 210 minutes. Then set up the rate with words on top and minutes on bottom:

$\dfrac{9,450\,\text{words}}{210\,\text{minutes}} = 45\,\text{words per minute}$

29. How to deal with TABLES, GRAPHS, AND CHARTS

Read the question and all labels extra carefully. Ignore extraneous information and zero in on what the question asks for. Take advantage of the spread in the answer choices by approximating the answer whenever possible.

30. How to count the NUMBER OF POSSIBILITIES

In most cases, you won't need to apply the combination and permutation formulas on the GRE. The number of possibilities is generally so small that the best approach is just to write them out systematically and count them.

Example: How many three-digit numbers can be formed with the digits 1, 3, and 5 used only once?

Setup: Write them out. Be systematic so you don't miss any: 135, 153, 315, 351, 513, 531. Count them: six possibilities.

31. How to calculate a simple PROBABILITY

$$Probability = \dfrac{Number\ of\ favorable\ outcomes}{Total\ number\ of\ possible\ outcomes}$$

Example: What is the probability of throwing a 5 on a fair six-sided die?

Setup: There is one favorable outcome—throwing a 5. There are 6 possible outcomes—one for each side of the die.

$Probability = \dfrac{1}{6}$

32. How to work with new SYMBOLS

If you see a symbol you've never seen before, don't freak out: it's a made-up symbol. Everything you need to know is in the question stem. Just follow the instructions.

33. How to SIMPLIFY POLYNOMIALS

First multiply to eliminate all parentheses. Each term inside one parentheses is multiplied by each term inside the other parentheses. All like terms are then combined.

Example: $(3x^2 + 5x)(x - 1) = 3x^2(x - 1) + 5x(x - 1) = 3x^3 - 3x^2 + 5x^2 - 5x = 3x^3 + 2x^2 - 5x$

34. How to FACTOR certain POLYNOMIALS

Learn to spot these classic factorables:

$$ab + ac = a(b + c)$$

$$a^2 + 2ab + b^2 = (a + b)^2$$

$$a^2 - 2ab + b^2 = (a - b)^2$$

$$a^2 - b^2 = (a - b)(a + b)$$

35. How to solve for one variable IN TERMS OF ANOTHER

To find x "in terms of" y: isolate x on one side, leaving y as the only variable on the other.

36. How to solve an INEQUALITY

Treat it much like an equation—adding, subtracting, multiplying, and dividing both sides by the same thing. Just remember to reverse the inequality sign if you multiply or divide by a negative quantity.

Example: Rewrite $7 - 3x > 2$ in its simplest form.

Setup: $7 - 3x > 2$

Subtract 7 from both sides: $7 - 3x - 7 > 2 - 7$. So $-3x > -5$.

Now divide both sides by -3, and remember to reverse the inequality sign:

$$x < \frac{5}{3}$$

37. How to handle ABSOLUTE VALUES

The *absolute value* of a number n, denoted by $|n|$, is defined as n if $n \geq 0$ and $-n$ if $n < 0$. The absolute value of a number is the distance from zero to the number on the number line:

$|-5| = 5$
If $|x| = 3$, then x could be 3 or -3.

Example: If $|x - 3| < 2$, what is the range of possible values for x?

Setup: $|x - 3| < 2$, so $(x - 3) < 2$ and $-(x - 3) < 2$. So $x - 3 < 2$ and $x - 3 > -2$. So $x < 2 + 3$ and $x > -2 + 3$. So $x < 5$ and $x > 1$. So $1 < x < 5$.

38. How to TRANSLATE ENGLISH INTO ALGEBRA

Look for the key words and systematically turn phrases into algebraic expressions and sentences into equations.

Here's a table of key words that you may have to translate into mathematical terms:

Operation	Key Words
Addition	sum, plus, and, added to, more than, increased by, combined with, exceeds, total, greater than
Subtraction	difference between, minus, subtracted from, decreased by, diminished by, less than, reduced by
Multiplication	of, product, times, multiplied by, twice, double, triple, half
Division	quotient, divided by, per, out of, ratio of __ to __
Equals	equals, is, was, will be, the result is, adds up to, costs, is the same as

39. How to find an ANGLE formed by INTERSECTING LINES

Vertical angles are equal. Adjacent angles add up to 180°.

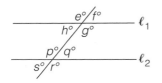

$$a = c$$
$$b = d$$
$$a + b = 180°$$
$$a + b + c + d = 360°$$

40. How to find an angle formed by a TRANSVERSAL across PARALLEL LINES

All the acute angles are equal. All the obtuse angles are equal. An acute plus an obtuse equals 180°.

Example:

ℓ_1 is parallel to ℓ_2

$$e = g = p = r$$
$$f = h = q = s$$
$$e + q = g + s = 180°$$

41. How to find the AREA of a TRIANGLE

$$Area = \frac{1}{2}(base)(height)$$

Example:

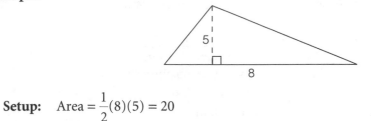

Setup: $Area = \frac{1}{2}(8)(5) = 20$

42. How to work with ISOSCELES TRIANGLES

Isosceles triangles have two equal sides and two equal angles. If a GRE question tells you that a triangle is isoceles, you can bet that you'll need to use that information to find the length of a side or a measure of an angle.

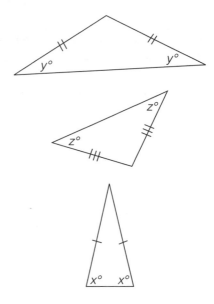

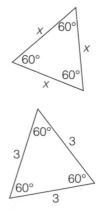

43. How to work with EQUILATERAL TRIANGLES

Equilateral triangles have three equal sides and three 60° angles. If a GRE question tells you that a triangle is equilateral, you can bet that you'll need to use that information to find the length of a side or a measure of an angle.

44. How to work with SIMILAR TRIANGLES

In similar triangles, corresponding angles are equal and corresponding sides are proportional. If a GRE question tells you that triangles are similar, you'll probably need that information to find the length of a side or the measure of an angle.

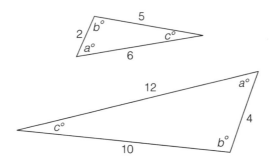

45. How to find the HYPOTENUSE or a LEG of a RIGHT TRIANGLE

Pythagorean theorem: $a^2 + b^2 = c^2$

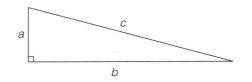

46. How to spot SPECIAL RIGHT TRIANGLES

      3-4-5

      5-12-13

      30-60-90

      45-45-90

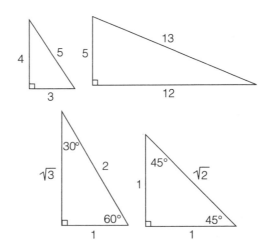

47. How to find the PERIMETER of a RECTANGLE

Perimeter = 2(length + width)

Example:

Setup: Perimeter = 2(2 + 5) = 14

48. How to find the AREA of a RECTANGLE

Area = (length)(width)

Example:

Setup: Area = 2 × 5 = 10

49. How to find the AREA of a SQUARE

Area = (side)²

Example:

Setup: Area = 3² = 9

50. How to find the AREA of a PARALLELOGRAM

Area = (base)(height)

Example:

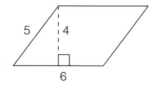

Setup: Area = 6 × 4 = 24

51. How to find the AREA of a TRAPEZOID

A trapezoid is a quadrilateral having only two parallel sides. You can always drop a line or two to break the figure into a rectangle and a triangle or two triangles. Use the area formulas for those familiar shapes. You could also apply the general formula for the area of a trapezoid:

Area = (Average of parallel sides) × (height)

Example:

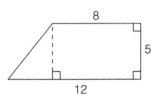

Setup: Area of rectangle = $8 \times 5 = 40$
Area of triangle = $\frac{1}{2}(4 \times 5) = 10$
Area of trapeziod = $40 + 10 = 50$

52. How to find the CIRCUMFERENCE of a CIRCLE

Circumference = 2πr

Example:

Setup: Circumference = $2\pi(5) = 10\pi$

53. How to find the AREA of a CIRCLE

Area = πr²

Example:

Setup: Area = $\pi \times 5^2 = 25\pi$

54. How to find the DISTANCE BETWEEN POINTS on the coordinate plane

If two points have the same xs or the same ys—that is, they make a line segment that is parallel to an axis—all you have to do is subtract the numbers that are different.

Example: What is the distance from (2, 3) to (−7, 3)?

Setup: The ys are the same, so just subtract the xs. $2 - (-7) = 9$

If the points have different xs and different ys, make a right triangle and use the Pythagorean theorem.

Example: What is the distance from (2, 3) to (−1, −1)?

Setup:

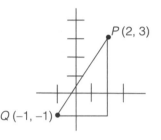

It's a 3-4-5 triangle!

$PQ = 5$

55. How to find the SLOPE of a LINE

$$Slope = \frac{rise}{run} = \frac{change\ in\ y}{change\ in\ x}$$

Example: What is the slope of the line that contains the points (1, 2) and (4, −5)?

Setup: Slope $\dfrac{-5-2}{4-1} = \dfrac{-7}{3}$

LEVEL 3 (MATH YOU MIGHT FIND DIFFICULT)

56. How to determine COMBINED PERCENT INCREASE/DECREASE

Start with 100 and see what happens.

Example: A price rises by 10 percent one year and by 20 percent the next. What's the combined percent increase?

Setup: Say the original price is $100.

Year one: $100 + (10\% \text{ of } 100) = 100 + 10 = 110$
Year two: $110 + (20\% \text{ of } 110) = 110 + 22 = 132$
From 100 to 132—That's a 32 percent increase.

57. How to find the ORIGINAL WHOLE before percent increase/decrease

Think of a 15 percent increase over x as $1.15x$ and set up an equation.

Example: After decreasing by 5 percent, the population is now 57,000. What was the original population?

Setup: $0.95 \times (\text{Original population}) = 57,000$ Original population $= 57,000 \div 0.95 = 60,000$

58. How to solve a SIMPLE INTEREST problem

With simple interest, the interest is computed on the principal only and is given by:

Interest = (principal) × (interest rate*) × (time**)

> * expressed as a decimal
> ** expressed in years

Example: If $12,000 is invested at 6 percent simple annual interest, how much interest is earned after 9 months?

Setup: $(12,000) \times (0.06) \times \left(\dfrac{9}{12}\right) = \$540$

59. How to solve a COMPOUND INTEREST problem

If interest is compounded, the interest is computed on the principal as well as on any interest earned. To compute compound interest:

$$(\textit{final balance}) = (\textit{principal}) \times \left(1 + \frac{\textit{interest rate}}{C}\right)^{(\textit{time})(C)}$$

where C = the number of times compounded annually

Example: If $10,000 is invested at 8 percent annual interest, compounded semiannually, what is the balance after one year?

Setup: Final balance.

$$= (10,000) \times \left(1 + \frac{0.08}{2}\right)^{(1)(2)}$$
$$= (10,000) \times (1.04)^2$$
$$= \$10,816$$

60. How to solve a REMAINDERS problem

Pick a number that fits the given conditions and see what happens.

Example: When n is divided by 7, the remainder is 5. What is the remainder when $2n$ is divided by 7?

Setup: Find a number that leaves a remainder of 5 when divided by 7. A good choice would be 12. If $n = 12$, then $2n = 24$, which, when divided by 7, leaves a remainder of 3.

61. How to solve a DIGITS problem

Use a little logic—and some trial and error.

Example: If A, B, C, and D represent distinct digits in the addition problem below, what is the value of D?

$$\begin{array}{r} AB \\ +BA \\ \hline CDC \end{array}$$

Setup: Two 2-digit numbers will add up to at most something in the 100s, so $C = 1$. B plus A in the units' column gives a 1, and since it can't simply be that $B + A = 1$, it must be that $B + A = 11$, and a 1 gets carried. In fact, A and B can be any pair of digits that add up to 11 (3 and 8, 4 and 7, etc.), but it doesn't matter what they are, they always give you the same thing for D:

$$
\begin{array}{r} 47 \\ +74 \\ \hline 121 \end{array}
\qquad\qquad
\begin{array}{r} 83 \\ +38 \\ \hline 121 \end{array}
$$

62. How to find a WEIGHTED AVERAGE

Give each term the appropriate "weight."

Example: The girls' average score is 30. The boys' average score is 24. If there are twice as many boys as girls, what is the overall average?

Setup:

$$
\text{Weighted avg.} = \frac{1 \times 30 + 2 \times 24}{3} = \frac{78}{3} = 26
$$

HINT: Don't just average the averages.

63. How to find the NEW AVERAGE when a number is added or deleted

Use the sum of the terms of the old average to help you find the new average.

Example: Michael's average score after four tests is 80. If he scores 100 on the fifth test, what's his new average?

Setup: Find the original sum from the original average: Original sum = $4 \times 80 = 320$

Add the fifth score to make the new sum: New sum = $320 + 100 = 420$

Find the new average from the new sum: New average $= \dfrac{420}{5} = 84$

64. How to use the ORIGINAL AVERAGE and NEW AVERAGE to figure out WHAT WAS ADDED OR DELETED

Use the sums.

Number added = (new sum) − (original sum)

Number deleted = (original sum) − (new sum)

Example: The average of five numbers is 2. After one number is deleted, the new average is −3. What number was deleted?

Setup: Find the original sum from the original average: Original sum = $5 \times 2 = 10$

Find the new sum from the new average: New sum = $4 \times (-3) = -12$

The difference between the original sum and the new sum is the answer. Number deleted = $10 - (-12) = 22$

65. How to find an AVERAGE RATE

Convert to totals.

$$Average\ A\ per\ B = \frac{Total\ A}{Total\ B}$$

Example: If the first 500 pages have an average of 150 words per page, and the remaining 100 pages have an average of 450 words per page, what is the average number of words per page for the entire 600 pages?

Setup: Total pages = 500 + 100 = 600 Total words = $500 \times 150 + 100 \times 450 = 120{,}000$

$$Average\ words\ per\ page = \frac{120{,}000}{600} = 200$$

To find an average speed, you also convert to totals.

$$Average\ speed = \frac{Total\ distance}{Time}$$

Example: Rosa drove 120 miles one way at an average speed of 40 miles per hour and returned by the same 120-mile route at an average speed of 60 miles per hour. What was Rosa's average speed for the entire 240-mile round trip?

Setup: To drive 120 miles at 40 mph takes three hours. To return at 60 mph takes two hours. The total time, then, is five hours.

$$Average\ speed = \frac{240\ miles}{5\ hours} = 48\ mph$$

66. How to solve a WORK PROBLEM

In a work problem, you are given the rate at which people or machines perform work individually and are asked to compute the rate at which they work together (or vice versa). The work formula states: the inverse of the time it would take everyone working together equals the sum of the inverses of the times it would take each working individually. In other words:

$$\frac{1}{r} + \frac{1}{s} = \frac{1}{t}$$

where r and s are, for example, the number of hours it would take Rebecca and Sam, respectively to complete a job working by themselves, and t is the number of hours it would take the two of them working together.

Example: If it takes Joe four hours to paint a room and Pete twice as long to paint the same room, how long would it take the two of them, working together, to paint the same room, if each of them works at his respective individual rate?

Setup: Joe takes four hours, so Pete takes eight hours; thus:

$$\frac{1}{4} + \frac{1}{8} = \frac{1}{t}$$
$$\frac{2}{8} + \frac{1}{8} = \frac{1}{t}$$
$$\frac{3}{8} = \frac{1}{t}$$
$$t = \frac{1}{\left(\frac{3}{8}\right)} = \frac{8}{3}$$

So it would take them $\frac{8}{3}$ hours, or 2 hours 40 minutes, to paint the room together.

67. How to determine a COMBINED RATIO

Multiply one or both ratios by whatever you need to in order to get the terms they have in common to match.

Example: The ratio of a to b is 7:3. The ratio of b to c is 2:5. What is the ratio of a to c?

Setup: Multiply each member of $a:b$ by 2 and multiply each member of $b:c$ by 3 and you get $a:b = 14:6$ and $b:c = 6:15$. Now that the bs match, you can just take a and c and say $a:c = 14:15$.

68. How to solve a DILUTION or MIXTURE problem

In dilution or mixture problems, you have to determine the characteristics of the resulting mixture when substances with different characteristics are combined. Or, alternatively, you have to determine how to combine substances with different characteristics to produce a desired mixture. There are two approaches to such problems—the straightforward setup and the balancing method.

Example: If five pounds of raisins that cost $1 per pound are mixed with two pounds of almonds that cost $2.40 per pound, what is the cost per pound of the resulting mixture?

Setup: The straightforward setup: $(\$1)(5) + (\$2.40)(2) = \$9.80$

The cost per pound is $n = \$\dfrac{9.80}{7} = \$1.40$

Example: How many liters of a solution that is 10 percent alcohol by volume must be added to 2 liters of a solution that is 50 percent alcohol by volume to create a solution that is 15 percent alcohol by volume?

Setup: The balancing method: make the weaker and stronger (or cheaper and more expensive, etc.) substances balance. That is: (percent/price difference between the weaker solution and the desired solution) × (amount of weaker solution) = (percent/price difference between the stronger solution and the desired solution) × (amount of stronger solution).

In this case: $n(15 - 10) = 2(50 - 15)$

$$n \times 5 = 2(35)$$

$$n = \frac{70}{5} = 14$$

So 14 liters of the 10 percent solution must be added.

69. How to solve a GROUP problem involving BOTH/NEITHER

Some GRE word problems involve two groups with overlapping members and possibly elements that belong to neither group. It's easy to identify this type of question because the words *both* and/or *neither* appear in the question. These problems are quite easy if you just memorize the following formula:

Group 1 + Group 2 + Neither − Both = Total

Example: Of the 120 students at a certain language school, 65 are studying French, 51 are studying Spanish, and 53 are studying neither language. How many are studying both French and Spanish?

Setup: 65 + 51 + 53 − Both = 120

169 − Both = 120

Both = 49

70. How to solve a GROUP problem involving EITHER/OR CATEGORIES

Other GRE word problems involve groups with distinct "either/or" categories (male/female, blue collar/white collar, etc.). The key to solving this type of problem is to organize the information in a grid.

Example: At a certain professional conference with 130 attendees, 94 of the attendees are doctors and the rest are dentists. If 48 of the attendees are women, and $\frac{1}{4}$ of the dentists in attendance are women, how many of the attendees are male doctors?

Setup: To complete the grid, each row and column adds up to the corresponding total:

	Doctors	Dentists	Total
Male	55	27	82
Female		9	48
Total	94	36	130

After you've filled in the information from the question, simply fill in the remaining boxes until you get the number you are looking for—in this case, that 55 of the attendees are male doctors.

71. How to work with FACTORIALS

You may see a problem involving factorial notation. If n is an integer greater than 1, then n factorial, denoted by $n!$, is defined as the product of all the integers from 1 to n. In other words:

$$2! = 2 \times 1 = 2$$
$$3! = 3 \times 2 \times 1 = 6$$
$$4! = 4 \times 3 \times 2 \times 1 = 24, \text{ etc.}$$

By definition, $0! = 1! = 1$.

Also note: $6! = 6 \times 5! = 6 \times 5 \times 4!$, etc. Most GRE factorial problems test your ability to factor and/or cancel.

Example: $\dfrac{8!}{6! \times 2!} = \dfrac{8 \times 7 \times 6!}{6! \times 2 \times 1} = 28$

72. How to solve a PERMUTATION problem

Factorials are useful for solving questions about permutations, i.e., the number of ways to arrange elements sequentially. For instance, to figure out how many ways there are to arrange seven items along a shelf, you would multiply the number of possibilities for the first position times the number of possibilities remaining for the second position, and so on—in other words: $7 \times 6 \times 5 \times 4 \times 3 \times 2 \times 1$, or $7!$.

If you're asked to find the number of ways to arrange a smaller group that's being drawn from a larger group, you can either apply logic or you can use the permutation formula:

$$_nP_k = \frac{n!}{(n-k)!}$$

where n = (# in the larger group) and k = (# you're arranging).

Example: Five runners run in a race. The runners who come in first, second, and third place will win gold, silver, and bronze medals respectively. How many possible outcomes for gold, silver, and bronze medal winners are there?

Setup: Any of the five runners could come in first place, leaving four runners who could come in second place, leaving three runners who could come in third place, for a total of $5 \times 4 \times 3 = 60$ possible outcomes for gold, silver, and bronze medal winners. Or, using the formula:

$$_5P_3 = \frac{5!}{(5-3)!} = \frac{5!}{2!} = 5 \times 4 \times 3 = 60$$

73. How to solve a COMBINATION problem

If the order or arrangement of the smaller group that's being drawn from the larger group does NOT matter, you are looking for the numbers of combinations, and a different formula is called for:

$$_nC_k \frac{n!}{k!(n-k)!}$$

where n = (# in the larger group) and k = (# you're choosing).

Example: How many different ways are there to choose three delegates from eight possible candidates?

Setup: $_8C_3 = \dfrac{8!}{3! \times 5!} = \dfrac{8 \times 7 \times 6 \times 5!}{3 \times 2 \times 1 \times 5!} = 56$

So there are 56 different possible combinations.

74. How to solve PROBABILITY problems where probabilities must be multiplied

Suppose that a random process is performed. Then there is a set of possible outcomes that can occur. An event is a set of possible outcomes. We are concerned with the probability of events.

When all the outcomes are all equally likely, the basic probability formula is:

$$Probability = \frac{Number\ of\ desired\ outcomes}{Number\ of\ possible\ outcomes}$$

Many hard probability questions involve finding the probability that several events occur. Let's consider first the case of the probability that two events occur. Call these two events A and B. The probability that both events occur is the probability that event A occurs multiplied by the probability that event B occurs given that event A occurred. The probability that B occurs given that A occurs is called the conditional probability that B occurs given that A occurs. Except when events A and B do not depend on one another, the probability that B occurs given that A occurs is not the same as the probability that B occurs.

The probability that three events A, B, and C occur is the probability that A occurs multiplied by the conditional probability that B occurs given that A occurred multiplied by the conditional probability that C occurs given that both A and B have occurred.

This can be generalized to n events, where n is a positive integer greater than 3.

Example: If two students are chosen at random to run an errand from a class with five girls and five boys, what is the probability that both students chosen will be girls?

Setup: The probability that the first student chosen will be a girl is $\frac{5}{10} = \frac{1}{2}$, and since there would be girls and five boys left out of nine students, the probability that the second student chosen will be a girl (given that the first student chosen is a girl) is $\}49\}$. Thus, the probability that both students chosen will be girls is $\frac{1}{2} \times \frac{4}{9} = \frac{2}{9}$.

Let's consider another example where a random process is repeated.

Example: If a fair coin is tossed four times, what's the probability that at least three of the four tosses will be heads?

Setup: There are two possible outcomes for each toss, so after four tosses there are $2 \times 2 \times 2 \times 2 = 16$ possible outcomes.

We can list the different possible sequences where at least three of the four tosses are heads. These sequences are:

HHHT

HHTH

HTHH

THHH

HHHH

Thus, the probability that at least three of the four tosses will come up heads is:

$$\frac{\text{Number of favorable outcomes}}{\text{Number of possible outcomes}} = \frac{5}{16}$$

We could have also solved this question using the combinations formula. The probability of a head is $\frac{1}{2}$ and the probability of a tail is $\frac{1}{2}$. The probability of any particular sequence of heads and tails resulting from four tosses is $\frac{1}{2} \times \frac{1}{2} \times \frac{1}{2} \times \frac{1}{2}$, which is $\frac{1}{16}$.

Suppose that the result of each of the four tosses is recorded in each of the four spaces.

_____   _____   _____   _____

Thus, we would record an H for heads or a T for tails in each of the four spaces.

The number of ways of having exactly three heads among the four tosses is the number of ways of choosing three of the four spaces above to record an H for heads.

The number of ways of choosing three of the four spaces is

$$_4C_3 = \frac{4!}{3!(4-3)!} = \frac{4!}{3!(1)!} = \frac{4 \times 3 \times 2 \times 1}{3 \times 2 \times 1 \times 1} = 4$$

The number of ways of having exactly four heads among the four tosses is 1.

If we use the combinations formula, using the definition that $0! = 1$, then

$$_4C_4 = \frac{4!}{4!(4-4)!} = \frac{4!}{4!(0)!} = \frac{4!}{4!(0)!}$$

$$= \frac{4 \times 3 \times 2 \times 1}{4 \times 3 \times 2 \times 1 \times 1} = 1$$

Thus, $_4C_3 = 4$ and $_4C_4 = 1$. So the number of different sequences containing at least three heads is $4 + 1 = 5$.

The probability of having at least three heads is $\frac{5}{16}$.

75. How to deal with STANDARD DEVIATION

Like mean, mode, median, and range, standard deviation is a term used to describe sets of numbers. Standard deviation is a measure of how spread out a set of numbers is (how much the numbers deviate from the mean). The greater the spread, the higher the standard deviation. You'll never actually have to calculate the standard deviation on Test Day, but here's how it's calculated:

- Find the average (arithmetic mean) of the set.
- Find the differences between the mean and each value in the set.
- Square each of the differences.
- Find the average of the squared differences.
- Take the positive square root of the average.

Although you won't have to calculate standard deviation on the GRE, you may be asked to compare standard deviations between sets of data, or otherwise demonstrate that you understand what standard deviation means.

Example: High temperatures, in degrees Fahrenheit, in two cities over five days:

September	1	2	3	4	5
City A	54	61	70	49	56
City B	62	56	60	67	65

For the five-day period listed, which city had the greater standard deviation in high temperatures?

Setup: Even without trying to calculate them out, one can see that City A has the greater spread in temperatures, and therefore the greater standard deviation in high temperatures. If you were to go ahead and calculate the standard deviations following the steps described above, you would find that the standard deviation in high temperatures for City $A = A = \sqrt{\frac{254}{5}} \approx 7.1$, while the standard deviation for City $B = \sqrt{\frac{74}{5}} \approx 3.8$.

76. How to MULTIPLY/DIVIDE POWERS

Add/subtract the exponents.

Example: $x^a \times x^b = x^{a+b}$

$2^3 \times 2^4 = 2^7$

Example: $\dfrac{x^c}{x^d} = x^{c-d}$

$\dfrac{5^6}{5^2} = 5^4$

77. How to RAISE A POWER TO A POWER TO AN EXPONENT

Multiply the exponents.

Example: $(x^a)^b = x^{ab}$

$(3^4)^5 = 3^{20}$

78. How to handle POWERS with a base of ZERO and POWERS with an EXPONENT of ZERO

Zero raised to any nonzero exponent equals zero.

Example: $0^4 = 0^{12} = 0^1 = 0$. Any nonzero number raised to the exponent 0 equals 1.

Example: $3^0 = 15^0 = (0.34)^0 = -345^0 = \pi^0 = 1$. The lone exception is 0 raised to the 0 power, which is *undefined*.

79. How to handle NEGATIVE POWERS

A number raised to the exponent $-x$ is the reciprocal of that number raised to the exponent x.

Example: $5^{-3} = \dfrac{1}{5^3} = \dfrac{1}{5 \times 5 \times 5} = \dfrac{1}{125}$

$n^{-1} = \dfrac{1}{n}$, $n^{-2} = \dfrac{1}{n^2}$, and so on.

80. How to handle FRACTIONAL POWERS

Fractional exponents relate to roots. For instance, $x^{\frac{1}{2}} = \sqrt{x}$.

Likewise, $x^{\frac{1}{3}} = \sqrt[3]{x}$, $x^{\frac{2}{3}} = \sqrt[3]{x^2}$, and so on.

Example: $4^{\frac{1}{2}} = \sqrt{4} = 2$

$(x^{-2})^{\frac{1}{2}} = x^{(-2)\left(\frac{1}{2}\right)} = x^{-1} = \dfrac{1}{x}$

81. How to handle CUBE ROOTS

The cube root of x is just the number that multiplied by itself three times (i.e., cubed) gives you x. Both positive and negative numbers have one and only one cube root, denoted by the symbol $\sqrt{3}$, and the cube root of a number is always the same sign as the number itself.

Example: $(-5) \times (-5) \times (-5) = -125,$ so $\sqrt[3]{-125} = -5$

$$\frac{1}{2} \times \frac{1}{2} \times \frac{1}{2} = \frac{1}{8}, \text{ so } \sqrt[3]{\frac{1}{8}} = \frac{1}{2}$$

82. How to ADD, SUBTRACT, MULTIPLY, and DIVIDE ROOTS

You can add/subtract roots only when the parts inside the $\sqrt{}$ are identical.

Example: $\sqrt{2} + 3\sqrt{2} = 4\sqrt{2}$

$\sqrt{2} - 3\sqrt{2} = -2\sqrt{2}$

$\sqrt{2} + \sqrt{3}$ cannot be combined.

To multiply/divide roots, deal with what's inside the $\sqrt{}$ and outside the $\sqrt{}$ separately.

Example: $(2\sqrt{3})(7\sqrt{5}) = (2 \times 7)(\sqrt{3 \times 5}) = 14\sqrt{15}$

$$\frac{10\sqrt{21}}{5\sqrt{3}} = \frac{10}{5}\sqrt{\frac{21}{3}} = 2\sqrt{7}$$

83. How to SIMPLIFY A RADICAL

Look for perfect squares (4, 9, 16, 25, 36…) inside the $\sqrt{}$. Factor them out and "unsquare" them.

Example: $\sqrt{48} = \sqrt{16} \times \sqrt{3} = 4\sqrt{3}$

$\sqrt{180} = \sqrt{36} \times \sqrt{5} = 6\sqrt{5}$

84. How to solve certain QUADRATIC EQUATIONS

Forget the quadratic formula. Manipulate the equation (if necessary) into the "＿＿＿ = 0" form, factor the left side, and break the quadratic into two simple equations.

Example: $x^2 + 6 = 5x$

$x^2 - 5x + 6 = 0$

$(x - 2)(x - 3) = 0$

$x - 2 = 0$ or $x - 3 = 0$

$x = 2$ or 3

Example: $x^2 = 9$

$x = 3$ or -3

85. How to solve MULTIPLE EQUATIONS

When you see two equations with two variables on the GRE, they're probably easy to combine in such a way that you get something closer to what you're looking for.

Example: If $5x - 2y = -9$ and $3y - 4x = 6$, what is the value of $x + y$?

Setup: The question doesn't ask for x and y separately, so don't solve for them separately if you don't have to. Look what happens if you just rearrange a little and "add" the equations:

$$5x - 2y = -9$$
$$\underline{-4x + 3y = 6}$$
$$x + y = -3$$

86. How to solve a SEQUENCE problem

The notation used in sequence problems scares many test takers, but these problems aren't as bad as they look. In a sequence problem, the nth term in the sequence is generated by performing an operation, which will be defined for you, on either n or on the previous term in the sequence. Familiarize yourself with sequence notation and you should have no problem.

Example: What is the positive difference between the fifth and fourth terms in the sequence 0, 4, 18, ... whose nth term is $n^2(n - 1)$?

Setup: Use the operation given to come up with the values for your terms:

$$n_5 = 5^2(5 - 1) = 25(4) = 100 \quad n_4 = 4^2(4 - 1) = 16(3) = 48$$

So the positive difference between the fifth and fourth terms is $100 - 48 = 52$.

87. How to solve a FUNCTION problem

You may see classic function notation on the GRE. An algebraic expression of only one variable may be defined as a function, f or g, of that variable.

Example: What is the minimum value of the function $f(x) = x^2 - 1$?

Setup: In the function $f(x) = x^2 - 1$, if x is 1, then $f(1) = 1^2 - 1 = 0$. In other words, by inputting 1 into the function, the output $f(x) = 0$. Every number inputted has one and only one output (although the reverse is not necessarily true). You're asked to find the minimum value, so how would you minimize the expression $f(x) = x^2 - 1$? Since x^2 cannot be negative, in this case $f(x)$ is minimized by making $x = 0$: $f(0) = 0^2 - 1 = -1$, so the minimum value of the function is -1.

88. How to handle GRAPHS of FUNCTIONS

You may see a problem that involves a function graphed onto the xy-coordinate plane, often called a "rectangular coordinate system" on the GRE. When graphing a function, the output, $f(x)$, becomes the y-coordinate. For example, in the previous example, $f(x) = x^2 - 1$, you've already determined two points, $(1, 0)$ and $(0, -1)$. If you were to keep plugging in numbers to determine more points and then plotted those points on the xy-coordinate plane, you would come up with something like this:

This curved line is called a *parabola*. In the event that you should see a parabola on the GRE (it could be upside down or more narrow or wider than the one shown), you will most likely be asked to choose which equation the parabola is describing. These questions can be surprisingly easy to answer. Pick out obvious points on the graph, such as (1, 0) and (0, −1) above, plug these values into the answer choices, and eliminate answer choices that don't jibe with those values until only one answer choice is left.

89. How to handle LINEAR EQUATIONS

You may also encounter linear equations on the GRE. A linear equation is often expressed in the form

$y = mx + b$, where:
- $m =$ the slope of the line $= \dfrac{rise}{run}$.

For instance, a slope of 3 means that the line rises 3 steps for every 1 step it makes to the right. A positive slope slopes up from left to right. A negative slope slopes down from left to right. A slope of zero (e.g., $y = 5$) is a flat line.

- $b =$ the y-intercept (where the line passes the y-axis).

Example: The graph of the linear equation $y = -\dfrac{3}{4}x + 3$ is:

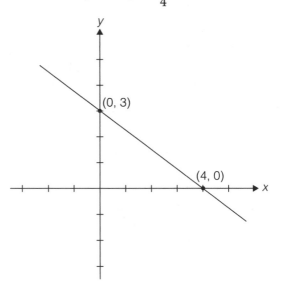

Note: The equation above could also be written in the form $3x + 4y = 12$.

To get a better handle on an equation written in this form, you can solve for y to write it in its more familiar form. Or, if you're asked to choose which equation the line is describing, you can pick obvious points such as (0, 3) and (4, 0) above, and use these values to eliminate answer choices until only one answer is left.

90. How to find the x- and y-INTERCEPTS of a line

The x-intercept of a line is the value of x where the line crosses the x-axis. In other words, it's the value of x when $y = 0$. Likewise, the y-intercept is the value of y where the line crosses the y-axis, i.e., the value of y when $x = 0$. The y-intercept is also the value b when the equation is in the form: $y = mx + b$. For instance, in the line shown in the previous example, the x-intercept is 4 and the y-intercept is 3.

91. How to find the MAXIMUM and MINIMUM lengths for a SIDE of a TRIANGLE

If you know n = the lengths of two sides of a triangle, you know that the third side is between the positive difference and the sum.

Example: The length of one side of a triangle is 7. The length of another side is 3. What is the range of possible lengths for the third side?

Setup: The third side is greater than the difference ($7 - 3 = 4$) and less than the sum ($7 + 3 = 10$).

92. How to find one angle or the sum of all the ANGLES of a REGULAR POLYGON

Sum of the interior angles in a polygon with n sides =

$(n - 2) \times 180$

Degree measure of one angle in a regular polygon with n sides =

$$\frac{(n-2) \times 180}{n}$$

Example: What is the measure of one angle of a regular pentagon?

Setup: Plug $n = 5$ into the formula: Degree measure of one angle =

$$\frac{(5-2) \times 180}{5} = \frac{540}{5} = 108$$

93. How to find the LENGTH of an ARC

Think of an arc as a fraction of the circle's circumference.

$$Length\ of\ arc = \frac{n}{360} \times 2\pi r$$

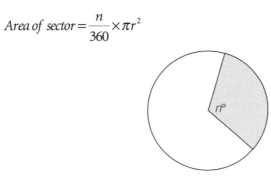

94. How to find the AREA of a SECTOR

Think of a sector as a fraction of the circle's area.

$$Area\ of\ sector = \frac{n}{360} \times \pi r^2$$

95. How to find the dimensions or area of an INSCRIBED or CIRCUMSCRIBED FIGURE

Look for the connection. Is the diameter the same as a side or a diagonal?

Example: If the area of the square is 36, what is the circumference of the circle?

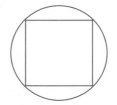

Setup: To get the circumference, you need the diameter or radius. The circle's diameter is also the square's diagonal, which (the diagonal creates two 45-45-90 triangles!) is 6$\sqrt{2}$.

Circumference $= \pi(diameter) = 6\pi\sqrt{2}$

96. How to find the VOLUME of a RECTANGULAR SOLID

Volume = length × width × height

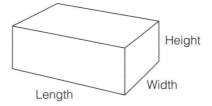

97. How to find the SURFACE AREA of a RECTANGULAR SOLID

To find the surface area of a rectangular solid, you have to find the area of each face and add them together. Here's the formula:

Surface area = 2(length × width + length × height + width × height)

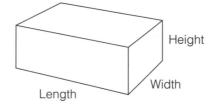

98. How to find the DIAGONAL of a RECTANGULAR SOLID

Use the Pythagorean theorem twice, unless you spot "special" triangles.

Example: What is the length of *AG*?

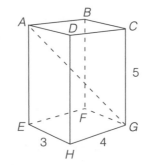

Setup: Draw diagonal *AC*.

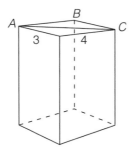

ABC is a 3-4-5 triangle, so *AC* = 5. Now look at triangle *ACG*:

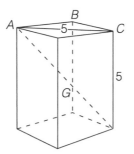

ACG is another special triangle, so you don't need to use the Pythagorean theorem. *ACG* is a 45-45-90, so *AG* = $5\sqrt{2}$.

99. How to find the VOLUME of a CYLINDER

Volume = $\pi r^2 h$

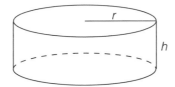

100. How to find the VOLUME of a SPHERE

Volume = $\dfrac{4}{3}\pi r^3$

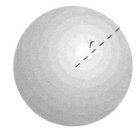

Getting into Grad School

You probably know what you want to study as a graduate student; but where will you apply? This question is usually a two-part question. First: which graduate programs should you consider, regardless of your chances? And second: which of these programs can you actually get into? This chapter will help you answer these questions—and many more you may have about the process of choosing an institution for postgraduate study.

WHAT PROGRAMS YOU SHOULD CONSIDER

Once you've made the decision to pursue graduate studies, the decision about where to go to school shouldn't be taken lightly. It will have a major influence on your daily life for the next several years and will influence your academic and career paths for years to come. Many students allow themselves to be influenced by a professor or mentor or school rankings, then find that they're unhappy in a certain program because of its location, workload, cost, or some unforeseen factor. With that said, remember: this is for your own good! Some hard work today will help to ensure that you'll be happy in your choice tomorrow. Let's take a look at some of the factors that you'll need to consider when choosing a school.

Your Goals

It's important to keep your goals in mind when evaluating graduate programs. Before you take the leap, it's key that you have a pretty clear idea where your interests really lie, what grad school life is like, and whether you are compatible with a particular program and its professors. Armed with this information, you should be able to successfully apply to the right programs, get accepted, and use your graduate school time to help you get a head start on the postgraduation job search.

Students decide to enter master's and doctoral degree programs for a variety of reasons. Some want to pursue a career in academia. To teach at two-year colleges, you'll need at least a master's degree; to teach and do research at four-year colleges, universities, and graduate programs, you'll need a doctorate. Others need graduate education to meet national and state licensing requirements in fields such as social work, engineering, and architecture. Some students want to change careers, while for others, an advanced degree opens up new opportunities in their current field.

Most master's programs are two years long, and master's students are generally one of two types: those on the academic track, where the degree programs focus on classical research and scholarship, and those on the practical track, where the degree program is actually a professional training program that qualifies them to enter or advance in a field such as social work or education.

Other options to consider if you're pursuing a master's degree are cooperative, joint, and interdisciplinary programs. In cooperative programs, you apply to, answer to, and graduate from one school, but you have access to classes, professors, and facilities at a cooperating school as part of the program. In joint- or dual-degree programs you work toward two degrees simultaneously, either within the same school or at two neighboring schools. Interdisciplinary programs are generally run by a faculty committee from a number of different departments. You apply to, register with, and are graduated by only one of the departments; you and your faculty committee design your curriculum.

Doctoral programs are designed to create scholars capable of independent research that will add new and significant knowledge in their fields. From the first, you will be regarded as an apprentice in your field. Your first year or two in the program will be spent on coursework, followed by "field" or "qualifying" exams. Once you've passed those exams, demonstrating that you have the basic factual and theoretical knowledge of your field down cold, you will then be permitted to move on to independent research, in the form of your doctoral dissertation. During most of this time you can get financial aid in the form of teaching or research assistantships; in exchange for assisting professors in the classroom or the lab, you get a small stipend and/or tuition remission.

If you want to get a doctoral degree, you can get a master's and reapply to Ph.D. programs, or enter directly into the doctoral program. The first method gives you flexibility but generally takes longer, costs more in the long run, and means reliving the application process.

Program Reputation

Although you shouldn't place too much stock in the school and program rankings, you should consider a program's overall reputation. When you assess a program's reputation, don't just consider its national ranking, but think about whether it fits your goals and interests. You can get information from a variety of sources, formal and informal.

Each year, various groups publish rankings of graduate programs: *U.S. News and World Report* on American graduate programs, *Maclean's* on Canadian programs, and many others. These rankings can give you a general sense of the programs in your field and may include profiles of distinguished professors, but they tell you nothing about departmental politics, job placement records, or financial aid possibilities.

You should find out which programs are highly regarded in the areas that interest you. You can learn about such details through professional associations (such as the American Psychological Association), comprehensive commercial directories of graduate programs (available through school or local libraries), and via the Internet.

Don't forget to contact schools and departments directly. Most departments have a chairperson who is also the admissions contact; he or she can put you in touch with current students and alumni who are willing to discuss the program with you. The chair is usually willing to answer questions as well.

Try to speak to at least one current student and one alumnus from each program you're seriously considering. You'll find that many graduate students are quite outspoken about the strengths and weaknesses of their professors, programs, and the state of the job market in their field.

If you're an undergraduate, or still have contacts from your undergraduate experience, ask your professors for their take on the various graduate programs. You'll often find that they have a great deal of inside information on academic and research trends, impending retirements, intellectual rivalries, and rising stars.

Remember, a program's reputation isn't everything, but the higher your school is regarded in the marketplace, the better your job prospects are likely to be upon graduation.

Location

The two key questions that you should consider regarding a school's location are: how will it affect the overall quality of your graduate school experience, and how will it affect your employability? Some students prefer an urban setting. Others prefer a more rustic environment. Cost of living can also be a factor.

Geography may be an important criterion for you. Perhaps your geographical choices are limited by a spouse's job or other family obligations. Or perhaps you already know where you want to live after graduation. If you're planning on a career in academia, you'll probably want to choose a nationally known program, regardless of where it's located. If, on the other hand, your program involves a practical dimension (psychology, social work, education, or some interdisciplinary programs), you may want to concentrate your school search on the area in which you hope to live and work, at least initially.

Curriculum

To maximize the value of your graduate school experience, be sure that a department's areas of concentration match up with your own interests. Knowing a program's particular theoretical bent and practical selling points can help ensure that you choose a school that reflects your own needs and academic leanings. Does one school of thought, one style of research, predominate? If so, is there anyone else working in the department with a different theoretical framework? Will you have opportunities to work within a variety of theories and orientations? What special opportunities are available? How well are research programs funded? Do the professors have good records at rounding up grants? In field or clinical work, what are the options? Are programs available in your area of interest?

Find the environment that works best for you. Don't put yourself in a situation in which you don't have access to the courses or training you're seeking. It's your education. Your time. Your energy. Your investment in your future. By being proactive, you can help guarantee that you maximize your graduate school experience.

Faculty

One of the most important decisions you make in your graduate school career will be your choice of adviser. This one person will help you with course selection, clinical, research, or field education opportunities, and can make or break the thesis/dissertation process. So when you investigate a department, look for a faculty member whose interests and personality are compatible with yours. Since this single person (your "dream adviser") may not be available, be sure to also look for a couple of other professors who, although their interests may not coincide exactly with yours, could work with you if you need them.

If one of your prime motivations in attending a certain program is to take classes from specific professors, make sure that you will have that opportunity. At the master's level, access to prominent professors is often limited to large, foundation-level lecture courses, where papers and exams are graded by the professor's graduate assistants or tutors. At the doctoral level, professors are generally much more accessible.

Is the department stable or changing? Find out whether the faculty is nearing retirement age. Impending retirements may not affect you in a two-year master's program, but this is a serious consideration in doctoral programs, which can (and often do) stretch on for over five years. If you have hopes of working with a distinguished professor, will he or she even be available for that time—and longer, if you are delayed? Will the department be large and stable enough to allow you to put together a good thesis or dissertation committee? Also try to find out whether younger members of the department are established. Do they get sufficient funding? Have they settled into the institution enough that there are not likely to be political controversies?

Placement

Although some people attend graduate school for the love of knowledge, most want to enhance their career prospects in some way. When you graduate with your hard-won degree, what are your chances of getting your desired job?

You'll want to ask what kind of track record a given program has in placing its alums. With today's highly competitive job market, it's especially important to find out when and where graduates have found work. If you're considering work in business, industry, local agencies, schools, health care facilities, or the government, find out whether these employers visit the campus to recruit. Major industries may visit science programs to interview prospective graduates. Some will even employ graduate students over the summers or part time. If you're going into academia, find out whether recent grads have been able to find academic posts, how long the search took, and where they are working. Are they getting tenure-track positions at reasonably prestigious departments, or are they shifting from temporary appointment to temporary appointment with little hope of finding a stable position?

Don't just look at the first jobs that a school's graduates take. Where are they in 5, 10, and even 25 years? Your career is more like a marathon than a sprint. So take the long view. A strong indicator of a program's strength is the accomplishments of its alumni.

Student Body

Some graduate catalogs contain profiles of or statements by current master's and Ph.D. students. Sometimes this is an informal blurb on a few students—it's really marketing material—and sometimes it's a full listing of graduate students. Use this as a resource both to find out what everyone else in the program is up to, and to find current students you can interview about the school and the program.

Because much of your learning will come from your classmates, consider the makeup of your class. A school with a geographically, professionally, and ethnically diverse student body will expose you to far more viewpoints than will a school with a more homogeneous group. If you're an older applicant, ask yourself how you will fit in with a predominantly younger group of students. For many, the fit is terrific, but for others, the transition can be tougher. The answer depends on you, but it's something to consider.

The student body, as well as the faculty, will have varied philosophical and political orientations. The theories and perspectives considered liberal in one program can be deemed conservative in another, and where you fit among your peers can have a great deal of influence on your image and your opportunities in your department. If you plan on an academic career, remember that your student colleagues will someday be your professional colleagues.

Networking

Forging relationships—with your classmates, your professors and, in a larger sense, all the alumni—is a big part of the graduate school experience. One of the things that you'll take with you when you graduate, aside from an education, a diploma, and debt, is that network. And whether you thrive on networking or consider it a four-letter word, it's a necessity. At some point it may help you advance your career, in academia or outside.

Quality of Life

Your graduate school experience will extend far beyond your classroom learning, particularly for full-time students. That's why it's so important to find out as much as you can about the schools that interest you. For example, what activities would you like to take part in? Perhaps convenient recreational facilities or an intramural sports program is appealing. If you'd like to be involved in community activities, perhaps there's a school volunteer organization. Regardless of your interests, your ability to maintain balance in your life in the face of a rigorous academic challenge will help you keep a healthy outlook.

Housing is another quality-of-life issue to consider. Is campus housing available? Is off-campus housing convenient? Is it affordable? Where do most of the students live?

Quality of life is also an important consideration for spouses and significant others, especially if school requires a move to a new city. When graduate school takes over your life, your spouse may feel left out. Find out what kind of groups and activities there are for partners. For example, are there any services to help your spouse find employment? Is child care available? Is there a good school system in the area?

Full-Time versus Part-Time

In a full-time program, you can focus your energy on your studies to maximize your learning. You're also likely to meet more people and forge closer relationships with your classmates. Many programs are oriented toward the full-time student and many top-tier programs don't offer part-time programs. A part-time schedule may also make it difficult for you to take classes with the best professors.

There are, however, many compelling reasons why attending part time may make sense for you. It may just not be economically feasible for you to attend full time. Or you may wish to continue gaining professional experience while earning the degree that will allow you to move on to the next level. If there is a possibility that you will have to work while you are in school, particularly while you're in the coursework stage, check out the flexibility of any program that interests you. Are there night/weekend classes? When is the library open? What about the lab? Talk to students who are currently in the program, especially those who work. Part-time programs often are slow, which can be discouraging, especially when licensure or salary increases are at stake.

Although many students in full-time graduate programs support themselves with part-time work, their primary allegiance is to the graduate degree. It will become the focus of your life, but if there is any way that you can manage full-time, or nearly full-time, studies at the higher levels, do it. You can graduate quicker and start picking up the financial pieces that much sooner—and often with a more secure base for your job search in the form of good support from your adviser.

Most master's programs are flexible about part-time studies, but doctoral programs are less so. Many doctoral programs expect a minimum amount of time "in residence"—that is, enrolled as a full-time student for a certain number of consecutive semesters. This requirement is usually listed in the catalog.

Program Costs

Some graduate programs charge "per credit" or "per hour," meaning that your tuition bill is calculated by the number of credits you take each semester. Other programs charge per semester or per year with a minimum and maximum number of credits you can take per semester for that flat fee. In general, per credit makes sense for part-time students while per semester makes sense for full-time students.

Generally speaking, the most expensive kind of graduate program (per semester) will be a master's degree at a private school. Loans are available to master's-level students, but grants, scholarships, and other forms of "free" financial assistance are harder to find. Furthermore, most private schools apply the same tuition rate to in-state and out-of-state residents. State colleges and universities usually give in-state residents a tuition break. Other forms of savings can come from finding the cheapest living and housing expenses and from working your way through the program as quickly as possible.

At the doctoral level, tuition remission (you don't pay any of it) and grants or stipends (they pay you) are common. Percentages of doctoral students in a program receiving full tuition remission plus stipend/grant money can range anywhere from 0 percent (although students in these programs may be receiving either tuition remission or stipend/grant money) to 100 percent— every student in the program pays no tuition and receives some grant or stipend. In these programs the major financial burden is living expenses over the years of coursework, language requirements, qualifying and field exams, research, and the dissertation.

WHERE YOU CAN GET IN

Now that you've developed a list of schools that meet your needs, you should take an objective look at your chances of getting into them.

Assessing Your Chances

A good way to get a sense of how graduate schools will perceive you is to make up a fact sheet with your GRE scores (or projected scores), your overall grade point average (GPA) as well as your GPA in your major, and your work experience. Outside activities and your personal statement will contribute to the overall "score" that admissions officers will use to evaluate you, but let's stick with the raw data for now.

The next step is to find a current source of information about graduate school programs. There are several guides published every year that provide data about acceptance rates for given years, median GPA, and GRE scores. You also can request this information directly from a given department. The school of your dreams may not care very much about your GPA, but it might be very interested in your GRE scores. Make sure you find out what your target school prioritizes in its search for worthy applicants.

One of the best ways to gauge whether you're in contention for a certain program is to compare your numbers to theirs. And remember that you needn't hit the nail on the head. Median means average, so some applicants do better or worse than the GRE scores or GPA cited. And, remember all those other factors that add up to make you a desirable applicant. Comparing numbers is merely a good way to get a preliminary estimate of your compatibility with the schools of your choice.

"Safety" Schools

Now that you have some idea of where you fall in the applicant pool, you can begin to make decisions about your application strategy. No matter what your circumstances, it's wise to choose at least one school that is likely to accept you, a "safety" school. Make sure it's one that fits your academic goals and your economic circumstances. If your GRE scores and GPA are well above a school's median scores, and you don't anticipate any problems with other parts of your record or application, you've probably found your safety school.

Top Choice Schools

If your ideal program is one that you don't seem qualified for, apply to your "dream school" anyway. You may be surprised! GPA and GRE scores are not the only two criteria by which applications are judged, and you may discover that you are admitted in spite of your academic background, on the merits of your personal statement, work samples, or other criteria. It's always worth a try. Some people underestimate their potential and only apply to safety schools. This can often lead to disappointment when they end up at one of these schools and discover that it doesn't provide the rigorous training that they want.

WHEN TO APPLY

With the number of graduate school applications received by institutions of higher learning on the rise, the issue of when to apply for admission has become very important. There are perfect times to begin and end the application process. You should begin at least a year before you plan to enter school (sooner if you're a nontraditional candidate or are changing fields). Find out the following essential dates as early as possible and incorporate them into your own personal application schedule:

- Standardized test registration deadlines
- Transcript deadlines (some schools send out transcripts only on particular dates)
- Letters of recommendation due dates
- Application deadlines (submit your application as early as possible to ensure that you get a fair and comprehensive review)
- Financial aid forms (federal/state programs, universities, and independent sources of aid all have definite deadlines)

Setting Up an Application Schedule

The following "seasonal" schedule is organized to help you understand how to proceed through the admissions process.

Winter (18–20 months prior to start date)

- If you're a nontraditional applicant or plan to switch fields, begin investigating program requirements. Take courses to make up any missing portion of your background.

Spring (16–18 months prior to start date)

- Browse through program catalogs and collect information on different grants and loans. Create your own graduate school library.

Summer

- Request applications from schools. If they're not available yet, ask for last year's so you can get a feel for the questions you'll have to answer.
- Write a draft of your personal statement and show it to trusted friends and/or colleagues for feedback.
- Consider registering for the GRE in the fall. This will give you plenty of time to submit your scores with your application.
- Research your options for test preparation. Take the test included in this book to give you a good idea of where you stand with regard to the GRE.

Early Fall

- Ask for recommendations. Make sure that your recommenders know enough about you to write a meaningful letter. Once your recommenders have agreed to write a recommendation, let them know when deadlines will be, so you can avoid any timing conflicts.

Late Fall

- Take the GRE.
- Request applications from schools, if you haven't already done so.
- Request institutional, state, and federal financial-aid materials from school aid offices.
- Request information on independent grants and loans.
- Order transcripts from your undergraduate (and any graduate) institution(s).

Winter

- Fill out applications. Mail them as early as possible.
- Fill out financial-aid applications. Mail these early as well.
- Make sure your recommendation writers have the appropriate forms and directions for mailing. Remind them of deadline dates.

Spring

- Sit back and relax (if you can). Most schools indicate how long they will take to inform you of their decision. This is also a crucial time to solidify your financial plans as you begin to receive offers of aid (with any luck).

The timing described here is rough, and you needn't follow it exactly. The most important thing for you to do is make yourself aware of strict deadlines well in advance, so that you'll be able to devote plenty of quality time to your application. Good luck!